Multilingual Capital

The languages of London's schoolchildren
and their relevance to economic, social and educational policies

edited by

Philip Baker and John Eversley

Battlebridge Publications
2000

Battlebridge Publications
Box 421, 37 Store St, London WC1E 7BS
tel. 020 7278 1246, fax 020 7636 5550

ISBN   1 903292 00 X

First published 2000

GIS development and mapping: Yasir Mohieldeen

Photography: Annie Bungeroth and Anthony Lam

Printed and bound in Great Britain by
Hobbs the Printers Ltd
Totton
Hampshire SO40 3YS

Contents

List of Maps

THE RIGHT HONOURABLE THE LORD MAYOR

ALDERMAN CLIVE MARTIN OBE TD DL

MANSION HOUSE · LONDON · EC4N 8BH

TELEPHONE 020 7626 2500   FACSIMILE 020 7623 9524   E-MAIL lord.mayor@corpoflondon.gov.uk

I am delighted to be able to write the foreword for this interesting study.

The City of London has for centuries been a major trading centre, first for Europe and later for the whole world. It has also been a place where political and economic refugees from many different nations and backgrounds settled. These people invariably brought their own languages to London, and although they eventually learned English, their own languages and culture continued to be reflected in business and this greatly contributed to the developing prosperity of the City, and over time to Greater London.

Today both the City and Greater London are places where people of diverse linguistic backgrounds still transact their business - but on a vastly grander scale. Prior knowledge of English is now normal for those coming from other countries to negotiate transactions, but knowledge of languages other than English remains vitally important. Increasingly, London is seen as a place where institutions and firms operating internationally want to locate because they have access to mother-tongue speakers of a wider range of languages than anywhere else in the world. Indeed this study estimates that there are some 300 different languages spoken in London. When the European Bank for Reconstruction and Development was set up in the capital there was a requirement for speakers of 38 different languages. All were found from within London.

This study tabulates and describes London's many ethnic groups and their languages. I commend it to anyone concerned with the government of London as well as those conducting business in the capital.

Introducing the Languages of London Project

Philip Baker & John Eversley

The main aims of the Languages of London Project have always been:

- to bring together data on the languages spoken by London's schoolchildren which are collected separately by the different local education authorities (LEAs) in Greater London;
- to analyse and publish the findings;
- to draw attention to the applications of this information for economic, social and educational policies;
- to encourage people to appreciate the positive aspects of bilingualism, the ability to move between two cultures; and
- to suggest ways in which data collection might be improved in future.

The Languages of London Project began as one small element in the Logosphere Programme[1] which David Dalby and Tony Allan launched with seed money from the School of Oriental and African Studies (SOAS; part of the University of London) in 1993. The principal aim of this wider research programme was to develop new methods of language mapping using Geographic Information Systems (GIS) techniques. Philip Baker, who participated in this from the start, was responsible for identifying existing sources of language census data and it was in the search for these that the existence of data collected from London schoolchildren came to the programme's attention.

A two-year grant from the Leverhulme Trust followed in 1994-96, enabling the Logosphere Programme to begin developing sophisticated methods of computerized mapping. The results included, among other things, maps of the complex linguistic situation in Mauritius and a new Language Map of Africa.[2] By comparison with these, the language data available on London schoolchildren did not seem to lend themselves readily to these new approaches. A major drawback was that almost all boroughs were only able or willing to provide a single set of figures for their borough as a whole, i.e. without information about the distribution of speakers within their boundaries (by, for example, postal sector). This severely limited the mapping possibilities and led to the project being considered as a low priority during the period of the Leverhulme grant. Nevertheless, the Logosphere team recognized that the project had two very important positive features. First, contacts with LEAs (local education authorities) left no doubt that the mapping of London's languages would be of immediate practical value to many people. Second, this would provide a seemingly unprecedented opportunity to pioneer urban language mapping.

A Logosphere workshop, held at SOAS in September 1997, included a presentation on the Languages of London Project and this attracted the attention of several newspapers and radio stations. This in turn led London First Centre to contact the project and to try to find a suitable sponsor for it. While these efforts did not immediately succeed, they did put the project into contact with both Pauline Irwin and her colleagues at the Economic Development Unit (EDU) of the Corporation of London, and the London Research Centre (LRC).

Meanwhile, a chance reunion of Philip Baker and John Eversley at Queen Mary and Westfield College (QMW; part of the University of London) led to an agreement to collaborate to produce this book which would both report on the languages of London and begin to explore the implications of the data. It also led to the Public Policy Research Unit at QMW providing a financial advance which enabled specimen maps to be produced in order to show potential sponsors what was possible. With the continuing cooperation of Tony Allan and the GIS expertise of Yasir Mohieldeen at SOAS, it was then possible to start designing and producing full colour language maps of London. At the same time, John Eversley set about identifying appropriate authors for the various articles included in this book.

The City of London Corporation's EDU had, for some time, been seeking funding for the project and, in the autumn of 1998, agreed to make an important contribution towards computing and map-making expenses and also to cover the costs of providing every LEA school and reference library with a free copy of this book. Further financial help was provided by London First Centre. The University of Westminster subsequently provided Baker with a half-time salary for six months to complete his work on the project in 1999.

The LRC had already provided support and advice to the project but, in 1999, its Director of Demographics and Statistics, Rob Lewis, not only conceived the idea of making three CD-ROMs of photographs illustrating aspects of multicultural London,[3] but also generously offered us their use in this book. These photographs are the work of Annie Bungeroth and Anthony Lam,[4] to whom we would like to express our gratitude.

Thanks are also due to Tanya Pascual for her work on the layout of the photographs and to Yasir Mohieldeen for the computer processing of these.

Finally we would like to emphasise that this book is not an end in itself but merely a beginning. The applications of the data presented here have yet to be fully understood, and there is every prospect of obtaining more and better data in the near future. We also hope that similar work will be carried out in other cities, in Britain and elsewhere.

---

[1] The name was later changed to Linguasphere.

[2] The GIS methodology for these was developed, respectively, by Mike Farmer and Yasir Mohieldeen. It is hoped that these will appear in 2000 in a volume dealing with new developments in language mapping but publication details have yet to be finalized.

[3] Enquiries about these CD-ROMs should be addressed to <info@london-research.gov.uk>

[4] These photographers may be contacted by e-mail at <photos_uk@yahoo.com>

The languages of London's schoolchildren

Philip Baker & Yasir Mohieldeen

1. Introduction[1]

The main aim of this article is to examine data on languages used in the homes of pupils at London's primary and secondary schools in order to establish how many children speak each of these. A further aim is to provide information which could lead to the collection of better data in future.

London comprises 32 boroughs and the City. Each of these is a Local Education Authority (LEA). In 1978, the Inner London Education Authority (ILEA) began conducting regular censuses of the numbers of pupils speaking languages other than English at home (cf Sinnott 1989a). Other surveys were also carried out at this time (Rosen & Burgess 1980, Linguistic Minorities Project 1986). Nothing similar was organized in the Outer London boroughs until after ILEA's abolition (1989). Schools in all London boroughs now collect data on the home languages of their pupils regularly but this does not guarantee that such information is available. Three boroughs do not collate their figures centrally while one does not do so every year.[2]

Except where otherwise indicated, figures cited below and given on the maps derive from the most recent information made available to the project by April 1999 (and generally relate to either 1998 or 1999). In all cases, figures are for children attending LEA schools only; children attending private schools are thus excluded from this survey.

The data relate to more than 850,000 school-children.[3] However, there were categories of responses – 3.26% of the total – whose language name could not be determined. (1) Those whose language name was given as an adjective derived from the name of a country (Nigerian, Ghanaian, etc.). Since there are about 400 different languages in Nigeria and perhaps 100 in Ghana, there was no way such responses could be associated with one particular language). (2) Those whose language name could not be traced in the Linguasphere index of more than 40,000 language, dialect and ethnic names (Dalby 1999). Some of these are probably typing errors while others may well be place-names. (3) Those for whom no language name was given. Children in all three categories were entered in the basefile as 'unclassified'. In most boroughs, the number of 'unclassified' is quite small but there are two where the proportion exceeds 10%: Hillingdon (21.8%) and Newham (15.85%).

2. An overview of the languages of London

Data supplied by the LEAs mentioned more than 350 language names, some of which were alternative names for the same language. No language name was mentioned or the names were unclassifiable for other reasons (see above) in 3.26% of the responses. Table 1 lists percentages for the leading languages.

Table 1
Home languages of London schoolchildren

rank	language name	percentage
1.	English	67.86%
2.	Bengali+Sylheti	4.51%
3.	Panjabi	3.32%
4.	Gujarati	3.19%
5.	Hindi/Urdu	2.91%
6.	Turkish	1.74%
7.	Arabic	1.23%
8.	†English-based Creoles	1.20%
9.	Yoruba	1.16%
10.	Somali	0.93%
11.	Cantonese	0.77%
12	Greek	0.71%
13.	Akan (Twi (Ashanti) + Fante)	0.67%
14	Portuguese	0.67%
15	French	0.63%
16	Spanish	0.61%
17.	Tamil	0.41%
18.	Farsi (=Persian)	0.37%
19.	Italian	0.28%
20.	Vietnamese	0.27%
21.	Igbo	0.22%
22.	†French-based Creoles	0.20%
23.	Tagalog	0.18%
24.	Kurdish	0.16%
25.	Polish	0.17%
26.	Swahili	0.12%
27.	Lingala	0.11%
28.	Albanian	0.10%
29.	Luganda	0.09%
30.	Gã	0.09%
31.	Tigrinya	0.09%
32.	German	0.09%
33.	Japanese	0.09%
34.	Serbian/Croatian	0.08%
35.	Russian	0.08%
36.	Hebrew	0.07%
37.	Korean	0.06%
38.	Pashto	0.05%
39.	Amharic	0.05%
40.	Sinhala	0.05%

† As discussed later in this article, the figures for both English- and French-based Creoles are unreliable and incomplete.

[1] We are grateful to David Dalby, John Eversley, Anthony Grant, Ian McCallum, Antony Sanderson and Marian Storkey for their helpful comments on earlier drafts of this article. Responsibility for any errors in the text is ours.

[2] Bromley and Havering do not collate figures centrally and so were unable to provide figures. For both boroughs, estimates derived from the figures for schoolchildren from ethnic minorities were used and apportioned to particular languages on the basis of the averages of the principal adjoining boroughs. While acknowledging the limitations of this strategy, it was felt better to use estimates than to exclude these boroughs from the survey. Redbridge also does not collate figures centrally but provided some information which enabled more reliable estimate to be made. Waltham Forest's figures are based on a survey conducted in 1994, no more recent data being available.

[3] The total figure, and base for percentages for London as a whole, is 896,743. This is distorted by the Newham figures which appear to exceed the actual number of pupils in that borough. However, the comparison of the percentages attributed to the different languages in 1999 is sufficiently similar those of previous years to suggest that, whatever the cause of the error, this has not greatly exaggerated the relative importance of any one language to the disadvantage of any other in that borough.

Since the rank order in Table 1 relates to languages spoken by pupils only it may differ from the order obtained if speakers of all ages are taken into account (see Storkey *this volume* for details). It is nevertheless interesting to compare Table 1 with Table 2 which lists languages which have the largest numbers of speakers in the world.

Table 2

Languages with the largest number of speakers in the world

Estimates for the year 2000[4]

(Where two figures are given, the first is the figure for the total number of competent speakers while the figure in brackets is limited to those whose primary language this is. Where a single figure is given it refers to the number of competent speakers regardless of whether this is their primary language.)

1.	Putonghua (Mandarin)	1000m	(800m)
2.	English	1000m	(400m)
3.	Hindi/Urdu	900m	(550m)
4.	Spanish	450m	(400m)
5.	Russian	320m	(170m)
6.	Arabic	250m	(200m)
7.	Bengali	250m	(190m)
8.	Portuguese	200m	(180m)
9.	Malay/Indonesian	160m	(50m)
10.	Japanese	130m	(120m)
11.	German	125m	(100m)
12.	French	125m	(90m)
13=	Panjabi	85m	
13=	Wu[5]	85m	
15.	Javanese	80m	
15.	Marathi	80m	
17=	Korean	75m	
17=	Vietnamese	75m	
19=	Italian	70m	
19=	Cantonese (Yue)[6]	70m	
19=	Tamil	70m	
19=	Telugu	70m	
23.	Turkish	60m	
24=	Min-nan[7]	55m	
24=	Swahili	55m	
26=	Ukrainian	45m	
26=	Xiang[8]	45m	
26=	Polish	45m	
26=	Gujarati	45m	
26=	Thai	45m	
31=	Hausa	40m	
31=	Kannada	40m	
31=	Farsi (Persian)	40m	
31=	Tagalog	40m	
31=	Malayalam	40m	
36=	Hakka	35m	
36=	Burmese	35m	
36=	Oriya	35m	
39=	Laotian+Isan	30m	
39=	Sundanese	30m	

Tables 1 and 2 show that 22 languages are common to both lists. Languages proportionately better represented in London than in the world as a whole are: the English-based Creoles (comprising several languages), Yoruba, Somali, Greek, Akan, Igbo, the French-based Creoles (again comprising several languages), Kurdish, Lingala, Albanian, Luganda, Gã, Tigrinya, Serbian/Croatian, Hebrew, Pashto, Amharic, and Sinhala. Languages proportionately better represented in the world than in London are the Chinese languages Putonghua, Wu, Min-nan, Xiang and Hakka; Malay/Indonesian, Javanese and Sundanese; the Indic languages Marathi and Oriya, and three of the Dravidian languages of southern India: Telugu, Kannada, Malayalam; Korean; Ukrainian; Thai; Hausa; Burmese; and Laotian+Isan.

Table 3 gives some indication of the demand for instruction in particular languages in London.

Table 3

Number of part-time day and evening courses offered in particular modern languages at all levels by public sector establishments in Greater London 1999-2000[9]

Rank	language	courses
1.	English language[10]	497
2.	French	474
3.	Spanish	389
4.	German	279
5.	Italian	276
6.	Japanese	86
7.	Arabic	81
8.	Russian	79
9.	[modern] Greek	75
10.	Portuguese (Brazilian 6, European 60)	66
11.	Putonghua (Mandarin)	65
12.	Turkish	37
13.	Hindi/Urdu (Hindi 13, Urdu 17)	30
14.	Dutch	28
15.	Polish	18
16.	Bengali (15)+Sylheti (1)	16
17=	Cantonese	13
17=	Irish Gaelic	13
19.	Swedish	12
20=	[modern] Hebrew	11
20=	Welsh	11
22.	Czech	10
23.	Panjabi	9
24.	Gujarati	8
25=	Danish	6
25=	Farsi (Persian)	6
25=	Norwegian	6
28=	Malay (2)/Indonesian (3)	5
28=	Swahili	5
30=	Hungarian	4
30=	Serbian/Croatian	4
32.	Scottish Gaelic	3
33=	Catalan, Cornish, Korean, Somali, Thai, Vietnamese, Yoruba each	2
40=	Albanian, Amharic, Basque, Belarusian, Bulgarian, Estonian, Hausa, Kurdish, Latvian, Lithuanian, Romanian, Shona, Slovene, Tamil, Ukrainian, Yiddish, Zulu each	1

---

[4] Figures are taken from Dalby (1999) but have been rounded to the nearest 5m.

[5] A Chinese language of the Yangtse Delta area.

[6] Yue is its usual Chinese name.

[7] A Chinese language also known as Fukien and Hokkien.

[8] A Chinese language spoken in Hunan and Guangxi.

[9] Figures are derived from Miller (1993).

[10] This is the total of courses offering "English language" (150) and "English for speakers of other languages"(347).

Comparison of Table 3 with Table 1 reveals some striking differences. Most of the courses on offer are for European languages, including four not listed in Table 1: Dutch, Irish Gaelic and Swedish.. Of the non-European languages represented in both tables, only Japanese, Arabic, and Hebrew occupy higher positions in Table 3 than in Table 1. African languages are particularly poorly represented, there being no courses available for the Akan languages, Igbo, Lingala, Luganda, Gã and Tigrinya.

The comparison of Tables 2 and 3 shows that courses are available in London in 26 of the 40 languages with the largest numbers of speakers in the world. Those for which courses are not available are Javanese, Tagalog, Burmese, Sundanese, Laotian+ Isan, four of the languages of China (Wu, Min-nan, Xiang and Hakka) and five of the languages of India (Marathi, Telugu, Kannada, Malayalam and Oriya).

If Table 3 is compared with the situation six years earlier (Miller 1993),[11] the order of the first four languages is the same but, if account is taken of the number of courses, Spanish has moved far ahead of German while Italian has closed up on German. Below these, Japanese has moved from 6th to 5th position, Arabic from 8th to 6th position, and Putonghua from 11th to 10th while Cantonese has fallen three places to 16th. The latter may be a consequence of the transfer of power in Hong Kong (overwhelmingly Cantonese-speaking) from Britain to China (where only Mandarin has official status). Russian, Greek, Turkish and Dutch have each fallen one place as a result of these changes.

3. Languages and dialects

One question which work on this project has often provoked is "how do you decide what is, and what is not, a language?". What is usually mean by this is: what is the difference between a language and a dialect? For linguists, who study the nature and structure of language, most languages can be divided into a number of dialects associated with different geographical areas and/or particular social or ethnic groups within the society where that language is spoken. Where one variety of a language is adopted as the model to be taught in schools and used in the media, this tends to be termed "the standard dialect" by the linguist. In other words, a dialect is a non-pejorative term for a geographical or social subdivision of a larger entity, a language. However, the data supplied to the project were collected by people who are not linguists and it has therefore been necessary to take account of the general public's views of what constitutes 'a language' and 'a dialect' in order to interpret these data correctly.

For many people, 'a language' has certain attributes such as a standard written form, a literature, and official status in a country or region; and any variety of speech lacking these attributes may be considered 'a dialect'. However, that a language need not have a written form is obvious when one considers that every spoken language had to exist before anyone devised a written form for it. Official status is not a necessary attribute either.

Breton has never had such status in France but it is as much a language as Welsh (which does have official status in Wales, formalized in 1967). Conversely, Letzeburgesch is the official language of Luxembourg but many German-speakers would probably regard this as a dialect of their language.

The main source of reference used here to determine the status of the language names supplied by the LEAs, and the inter-relationships of these languages, is Dalby (1999) which is the most comprehensive classification of all the world's languages and dialects yet undertaken. A particular feature of this classification is that three layers of language are recognised – outer languages, inner languages, and dialects. Danish, Norwegian and Swedish, for example, are closely related and are classified as three of the inner languages which collectively form one outer language which he terms Nordic-East. In this article, both inner and outer language names are used depending on a variety of factors including: (a) the nature of the data provided, (b) which names are most familiar to readers, and (c) the attitude of speakers of the language(s) concerned. With regard to Danish, Norwegian and Swedish, (a), (b) and (c) all favour treating these separately. However, in the case of the Akan languages of Ghana, four different terms are used by the different LEAs: Akan, Ashanti, Fante and Twi. Dalby classifies Ashanti as one of the dialects of Twi. Twi and Fante are both classified as inner languages which together constitute the Akan outer language. Since some boroughs give figures for Akan, and these could only be divided arbitrarily between Fante and Twi, it seems preferable to combine all the figures and use the outer language name, Akan (which is known to be acceptable to speakers of all these varieties).

In Dalby's view, the world's languages form a continuum of human communication. Within that continuum, he identifies five phylosectors or major "language families". All languages not classified in one of the five phylo-sectors are assigned by geographical proximity to one of the five geosectors. Each sector is further divided into ten zones of reference. The basic scheme, covering all the world's languages and dialects is set out in Table 4 (overleaf).

In Table 4, the geosectors are numbered 0, 2, 4, 6 and 8 while the phylosectors are numbered 1, 3, 5, 7 and 9. For referential purposes, every phylosector is divided into ten phylozones, covering part or parts of the relevant language families. Each geosector is likewise divided into ten zones, which are either phylozones, each covering an isolated group of inter-related languages, or geozones, each covering a geographical grouping of apparently unrelated languages. Each of the ten zones into which each sector is divided has two digits, with a name ending in -ic only if it is a phylozone. For example, the zones 50 CELTIC, 51 ROMANIC, 52 GERMANIC, 53 SLAVONIC etc. are listed under phylosector 5 INDO-EUROPEAN. To the right of these are listed all the languages in each zone currently known to be spoken in London. Note that nine of the ten sectors, as well as 54 of the 100 zones, are represented in London.

---

[11]   The two are not strictly comparable because the 1993-94 edition of *Floodlight* (Miller 1993) excludes outer London boroughs.

Table 4

The Linguasphere

Ten Sectors each comprising Ten Zones†

Five Geosectors Fifty Zones		Languages in each zone spoken by some London schoolchildren	Five Phylosectors Fifty Zones		Languages in each zone spoken by some London schoolchildren
0	AFRICA		1	AFROASIAN	
00	MANDIC	Kono, Kpelle, Malinke, Mandingo, Mende, *Nwa	10	TAMAZIC	Berber
01	SONGHAIC		11	COPTIC	
02	SAHARIC		12	SEMITIC	Amharic, Arabic, Aramaic, Harari, Hebrew, Maltese, Tigray, Tigre
03	SUDANIC	Lugbara, Ma'di, Mangbetu	13	BEJIC	Beja
04	NILOTIC	Acholi, *Alur, A-Teso, Dhopadhola, Dinka, Kakwa, Lango, Luo/Lwo, *Nuer, Oromo, Shilluk	14	CUSHITIC	'Afar, Rendille, Saho, Sidamo, Somali
05	*EAST-SAHEL*	Nubian	15	EYASIC	
06	*KORDOFANIC*		16	OMOTIC	
07	*RIFT-VALLEY*		17	CHARIC**	
08	KHOISANIC	Damara	18	MANDARIC	*Bata
09	*KALAHARI*		19	BAUCHIC	Hausa, Tangale
2	AUSTRALASIA		3	AUSTRONESIAN	
20	*ARAFURA*		30	FORMOSIC	
21	*MAMBERAMO*		31	HESPERONESIC	Bisayan, Cebuano, Hiligay-non, Ilocano, Malagasy, Malay/Indonesian, Pampangan, *Pangasinan, Tagalog
22	MADANGIC		32	MESONESIC	
23	OWALAMIC		33	HALMAYAPENIC	
24	TRANSIRIANIC	Itigo	34	NEOGUINEIC	Motu
25	*CENDRAWASIH*		35	MANUSIC	
26	*SEPIK-VALLEY*		36	SOLOMONIC	Hahon
27	*BISMARCK-SEA*	Baining	37	NEOCALEDONIC	
28	*NORTH-AUSTRALIA*		38	WEST-PACIFIC	Kusaie, Nauruan,
29	*TRANSAUSTRALIA*		39	TRANSPACIFIC	Fijian, Hawaiian, Maori, Tongan
4	EURASIA		5	INDO-EUROPEAN	
40	EUSKARIC	Basque	50	CELTIC	Irish Gaelic, Scottish Gaelic, Shelta, Welsh
41	URALIC	Estonian, Finnish, Hungarian	51	ROMANIC	Catalan, French, French-based Creoles, Italian, Moldavian, Portuguese, Portuguese-based Creoles, Romanian, Spanish
42	*CAUCASUS*	*Abkhaz, Georgian	52	GERMANIC	Afrikaans, Danish, Dutch, English, English-based Creoles, Flemish, German, Icelandic, Krio, Norwegian, Swedish, *Swiss German, Tok Pisin, Yiddish

4 EURASIA *continued*

43	*SIBERIA*	
44	*TRANS-ASIA*	Azeri, Kazakh, Kirghiz, Mongolian, Turkish, Turkmen, Uzbek
45	*EAST-ASIA*	Japanese, Korean
46	*SOUTH-ASIA*	*Burushaski, *Khasi, Khmer, Korku, Vietnamese, Wa
47	*DAIC*	Lao, Lati, Thai
48	*MIENIC*	
49	*DRAVIDIC*	*Kannada, Malayalam, *Parji, Tamil, Telugu, *Turi

5 INDO-EUROPEAN *continued*

53	SLAVONIC	Belorussian, Bulgarian, Czech, Macedonian, Polish, Russian, Serbian/Croatian, Slovak, Slovene, Ukranian
54	BALTIC	Latvian, Lithuanian
55	ALBANIC	Albanian
56	HELLENIC	Greek
57	ARMENIC	Armenian
58	IRANIC	Balochi, Dari, Farsi, Kurdish, Pashto
59	INDIC	Assamese, Bengali, *Bihari, *Dhivehi, Gujarati, Hindi/Urdu, Kachchhi, Kashmiri, Konkani, Marathi, Nepali, Oriya, Panjabi, Rajasthani, Romany, Sindhi, Sinhala, Sylheti

6 NORTH-AMERICA

60	*ARCTIC*
61	*NADENIC*
62	*ALGIC*
63	*SAINT-LAWRENCE*
64	*MISSISSIPPI*
65	*AZTECIC*
66	*FARWEST*
67	*DESERT*
68	*GULF*
69	*MESOAMERICA*

7 SINO-INDIAN

70	TIBETIC	Jonkha, Tibetan
71	HIMALAYIC	Newari
72	GARIC	
73	KUKIC	
74	MIRIC	
75	KACHINIC	Jingpho
76	RUNGIC	
77	IRRAWADDIC	Burmese
78	KARENIC	*Karen
79	SINITIC	Cantonese, Hakka, Min-nan, Putonghua (Mandarin)

8 SOUTH-AMERICA

80	*CARIBIC*	Carib
81	*INTER-OCEAN*	
82	*ARAWAKIC*	
83	*PRE-ANDES*	
84	*ANDES*	Quechua
85	*CHACO-CONE*	
86	*MATO-GROSSO*	
87	*AMAZON*	
88	*TUPIC*	
89	*BAHIA*	

9 TRANSAFRICAN

90	ATLANTIC	Fula, Limba, Wolof
91	VOLTAIC	*Bariba, Bimoba, *Dagari, Dagbane, Gurenge, Gurma, Mampruli
92	ADAMAWIC	Mbum
93	UBANGIC	*Zande
94	MELIC	Gola, Kisi, Temne
95	KRUIC	Bassa, Kru
96	AFRAMIC	Abe, Adangme, Akan (Ashanti, Fante, Twi), Akpafu, Efutu, Ewe, Fon, Gã, *Gonja, *Kposo, *Krobo, Logba, Nzema
97	DELTIC	Ijo, Kalabari, Nembe, Okrika
98	BENUIC	Abua, Anaang, Che, Ebira, Edo. Efik/Ibibio, *Eggon, Eleme, *Emai, Esan, Gokana, Gora, Idoma, *Idon, Igala, Igbo, Igede, Ikwere, Isoko, Itsekiri, Kaje, Katab, *Khana, Ki, Lam-nso, Ogori, Olulumo, Ora, Oring, Ukaan, Urhobo, Yoruba
99	BANTUIC	Ambo, Bemba, Bende, Bukusu, Chewa, Chiga, Chokwe, Ewondo, Fang, Gikuyu, Gogo, Herero, Kahe, *Kamba, *Kimeru, Kingwana, Kirundi, Kongo, *Kwangwa, Lingala, *Logoli, *Losengo, Lozi, Luba, Luganda, Lunda, Lusoga, *Luvale, Luziba, *Mambwe, *Masaba, Mungaka, Ndebele, Nsenga, Nyakyusa, Nyang, Nyoro, Oshiwambo, Runyankore, Rutoro, Rwanda, Senga, Shona, Sotho, Swahili, Swazi, Tiv, Tonga, Tswana, Tumbuka, Xhosa, Zulu

* Languages following an asterisk were reported in 1993-97 but not in the present survey.
** Not to be confused with Chadic (of which Charic, from the name of the river Chari, is part).

+ For full details of this referential classification, see Dalby (1999).
++ Geographic zones (geozones) are written in upper-case italics, e.g. *EAST-SAHEL*.

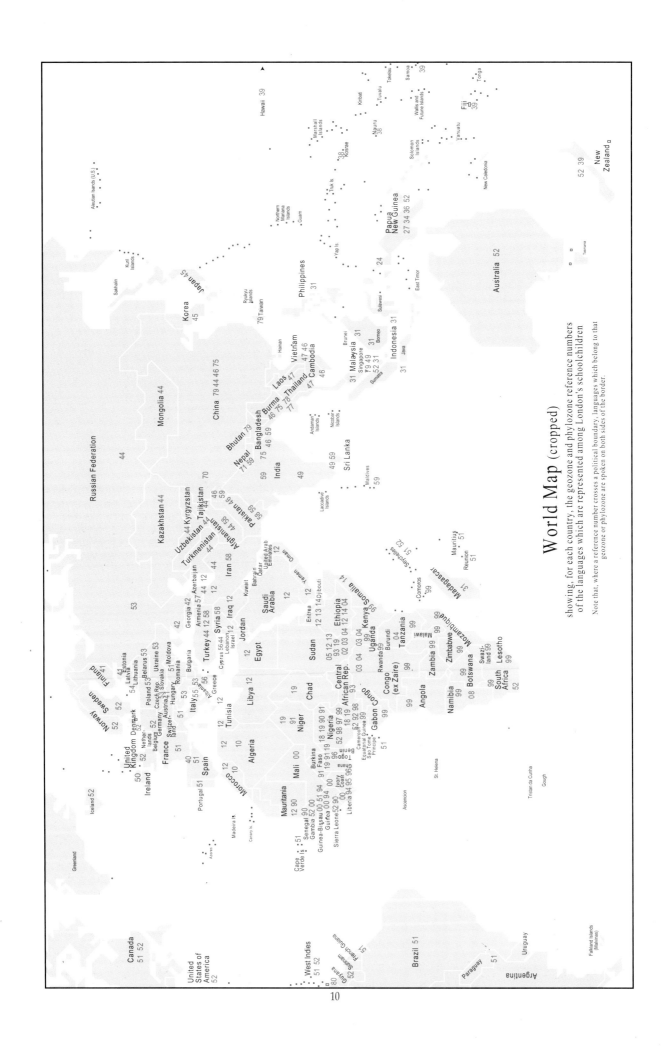

World Map (cropped)

showing, for each country, the geozone and phylozone reference numbers
of the languages which are represented among London's schoolchildren

Note that, where a reference number crosses a political boundary, languages which belong to that
geozone or phylozone are spoken on both sides of the border.

The world map (opposite) gives geozone and phylozone reference numbers for the languages of each country which are represented in London.[12] The numbers 44, 12 and 58 appear on the map of Turkey, for example. Comparison with Table 4 shows that these relate to Turkic (44 Turkish), Semitic (12 Aramaic) and Iranic (58 Kurdish). Note that 58 crosses its borders because Kurdish is also spoken in Syria, Iraq and Iran.

4. Mapping individual languages

Maps showing the spread across London of a selection of the capital's languages are interspersed at convenient places in the alphabetical list of languages which follows. As indicated above, all percentages on the maps relate to schoolchildren from homes in which these languages are spoken, rather than to the total population living in the same areas. There can be important differences between these two things, as Marian Storkey's article (*this volume*, pp 63-66) indicates.

The maps which follow were made in the Department of Geography at SOAS. Most of these maps are of Greater London divided into 33 LEAs. There are also four maps of individual boroughs: two of Westminster and two of Haringey. These borough maps are divided into postal sectors. The same colour/density scale is used on all maps.

On the maps of Greater London, LEAs in which the percentage of speakers of particular languages is greater than the average *for that language* for the whole of London are surrounded by a blue border. It is interesting to note that the above-average areas for particular languages are generally adjoining boroughs. This suggests that people choose to live in areas where they can maintain easy contact with others who speak their language and share their culture. This is perhaps what would be expected of groups who arrived in London in comparatively recent times (say, during the past 25 years) but it also seems to apply to those who came far earlier. In the text which accompanies the Alphabetical list of languages, attention will also be drawn to those boroughs in which the percentage speaking a particular language is five or more times greater than the average for London as a whole since this indicate areas of an unusually high concentration.

Another point of interest is that the local authority area with the highest percentage of speakers of each language is in most cases located north of the Thames. It is not clear why this should be so but transport facilities would seem to play some part in this, given that most major railway stations and Underground lines are situated north of the river.

Table 5 (overleaf) lists the three languages (other than English) with the highest proportion of speakers in each LEA. Note that the figures vary enormously. For example, 5.45% is only enough to secure Gujarati third place in Ealing while, in Sutton, 0.79% is sufficient to give Gujarati first place. Hindi/Urdu is mentioned more than any other language, occupying first, second or third place in 17 of the 33 LEAs.

5. Listing the languages of London

5.1 Introduction

Information on the classification of languages (i.e. how they are related to other languages), their location in the world, and their numbers of speakers is drawn primarily from Dalby (1999). Figures for the latter "include an allowance where appropriate for estimated totals of competent second-language speakers" (p 1).[13]

The total number of languages in the world depends very much on the definition of "language" which is adopted. However, Dalby's recognition of two levels enables us to think of this as ranging from nearly 5,000 "outer languages" to more than 13,000 "inner languages". Most of the ca. 300 names for which entries are given below are those of outer or inner languages but, in a few cases, such as Kurdish, they refer to two or more related outer languages.

Many languages are known and/or recorded under more than one name. Preferred language names are written in ***bold italics***. In most cases, there are important reasons for preferring one name or spelling over another. For example, the **g** and **b** in the name ***Igbo*** are pronounced simultaneously in that language; to write this as *Ibo* or *Ebo* is to misrepresent the language's name. In a few cases, there is little reason for preferring one name over another but, to avoid repeating entries, one has to be chosen over the other. *Persian* has been the usual name in English for the principal language of the country today known as Iran for many centuries and there is no obvious reason to change this. However, more LEAs currently prefer to term this ***Farsi*** and the latter name has been used on this occasion.[14] ("Farsi" is the name of this language in Persian so this is in effect the equivalent of referring to French as "Français".)

Language names which follow an asterisk are those which have been reported by one or more borough since 1993 even though they are not represented in the current survey. Language names not followed by an asterisk are recorded in this survey and their entries include the number of children reported as speaking them together with the name of the LEA where the largest number of their speakers is found within square brackets, e.g. [This survey: 295 speakers (53 Hillingdon)]. Note that 'speakers' here only refers to the schoolchildren reported and thus excludes the adults in their household. This is of course entirely separate from any figure indicating the total number of speakers of this language elsewhere in the world, often amounting to millions, which is sometimes given earlier in the entry.

Each entry includes the name of the phylozone or geozone to which each language or group of languages belongs, written in bold typeface. For further information about this, see Table 4 and the text which immediately precedes and follows that.

---

[12] Adapted from United Nations, Dept of Public Information, Cartographic Section, map no. 3933, rev. 2, Aug 1999; see <www.un.org/Depts/Cartographic/english/htmain.htm>.

[13] As Dalby (1999) says, figures for first-language speakers only can often give a misleading impression of their importance. For example, there are only about 6 million first-language speakers of Swahili but the figure rises to 55 million if one adds competent second-language speakers.

[14] Some LEAs also record this language as Irani or Iranian.

Table 5

Linguistic characteristics of local education authority areas

The three languages (other than English) spoken in the homes of the highest percentage of pupils in each LEA area

Local Education Authority area	Language 1	Language 2	Language 3
Barking & Dagenham	Panjabi 2.50%	Hindi/Urdu 1.60%	Turkish 0.50%
Barnet	Gujarati 5.95%	Greek 2.18%	Hindi/Urdu 1.50%
Bexley	Panjabi 3.42%	Cantonese 1.28%	Turkish 1.01%
Brent	Gujarati 23.85%	Hindi/Urdu 6.48%	Somali 3.89%
Bromley†	Panjabi 1.46%	Hindi/Urdu 0.63%	Cantonese 0.57%
Camden	Bengali+Sylheti 12.67%	Somali 2.38%	Spanish 1.82%
City of London	Bengali+Sylheti 56.37%	English Creole 6.86%	Japanese 3.43%
Croydon	Hindi/Urdu 1.49%	Gujarati 1.45%	French 0.76%
Ealing	Panjabi 20.12%	Hindi/Urdu 9.63%	Gujarati 5.45%
Enfield	Turkish 7.16%	Greek 4.80%	Gujarati 1.85%
Greenwich	Panjabi 9.40%	Yoruba 6.25%	Turkish 4.80%
Hackney	Turkish 10.61%	Yoruba 6.79%	Bengali+Sylheti 5.41%
Hammersmith & Fulham	Arabic 5.20%	Hindi/Urdu 2.07%	Somali 1.97%
Haringey	Turkish 9.99%	Akan 3.57%	Somali 2.72%
Harrow	Gujarati 18.80%	Hindi/Urdu 2.38%	Panjabi 1.67%
Havering†	Panjabi 0.36%	Hindi/Urdu 0.32%	Gujarati 0.09%
Hillingdon	Panjabi 6.49%	Hindi/Urdu 1.89%	Gujarati 1.71%
Hounslow	Panjabi 15.90%	Hindi/Urdu 7.59%	Gujarati 4.76%
Islington	Bengali+Sylheti 5.67%	Yoruba 2.42%	Greek 1.56%
Kensington & Chelsea	Arabic 9.72%	Portuguese 4.27%	Spanish 3.91%
Kingston upon Thames	Korean 0.83%	Tamil 0.66%	Arabic 0.35%
Lambeth	Yoruba 6.41%	Portuguese 4.08%	Spanish 2.12%
Lewisham	English Creole 29.78%	Cantonese 2.19%	French 1.96%
Merton	Hindi/Urdu 2.85%	Akan 1.91%	Tamil 1.88%
Newham	Bengali+Sylheti 10.97%	Hindi/Urdu 8.95%	Panjabi 7.24%
Redbridge	Hindi/Urdu 4.41%	Panjabi 4.38%	Gujarati 1.22%
Richmond upon Thames	Panjabi 1.04%	Gujarati 0.84%	Arabic 0.80%
Southwark	Yoruba 7.54%	Bengali+Sylheti 2.45%	Cantonese 2.06%
Sutton	Gujarati 0.79%	Hindi/Urdu 0.66%	Tagalog 0.38%
Tower Hamlets	Bengali+Sylheti 53.81%	Somali 1.19%	Cantonese 1.04%
Waltham Forest	Hindi/Urdu 8.82%	Panjabi 7.82%	Gujarati 2.38%
Wandsworth	Hindi/Urdu 4.69%	Gujarati 2.41%	Bengali+Sylheti 1.24%
Westminster	Arabic 12.48%	Bengali+Sylheti 11.84%	Portuguese 3.76%

† Estimated figures.

A list of territories and languages is given at the end of this article as an appendix (pp 59-60). Names of territories are arranged alphabetically, followed in each case by the names of languages of that country reported as being currently or recently spoken in London. The list of languages for Nigeria, for example, thus includes only those of the 44 reported in London rather than all 400 languages known to be spoken in that country. Language names follow zone numbers on which further information can be found on pp 7-11 (above).

5.2 Writing systems

Most of the world's languages are today written with the Roman alphabet. Where the languages listed below employ some other script, details are given in their entries. The writing systems of the world can be divided into five main groups: alphabetic, consonantal, syllabic, semi-syllabic, and logographic.[15]

POSTER FOR AN AFRICAN CONFERENCE IN SEVEN LANGUAGES: TIGRINYA (Ethiopic semi-syllabic script), ENGLISH, HAUSA, SWAHILI, FRENCH, ZULU (Roman alphabet) AND ARABIC (consonantal script).

Broadly speaking, alphabetic writing systems have a single letter for each contrastive sound in the language. The most extensively used of these systems is the Roman alphabet of 26 letters, often augmented by the use of diacritics ('accents' or marks added to a letter) e.g. French ç, é and è; German ü, ö and ä, Portuguese ã, Spanish ñ, etc. Apart from Roman, the only alphabetic system applied to many languages is Cyrillic, used for Russian, several related Slavonic languages and, often with some additional letters, a number of non-Slavonic languages spoken in the former USSR. Other alphabetic systems are, today at least, largely restricted to a single language such as Greek or Armenian.

Consonantal scripts were designed originally for Semitic languages such as Arabic and Hebrew in which the basic meaning of most words can be determined in context by a sequence of three consonants, thus limiting the usefulness of marking the vowels. Provision is made for vowels to be indicated by diacritics but these are normally written

only in texts intended to be read aloud (such as the Quran). However, where non-Semitic languages – such as Farsi and Hindi/Urdu, in which vowels play a much more important role in word recognition – are written in the Arabic script, vowels are always marked. Additional diacritics are often used to indicate the full range of vowels, and also for consonants not found in Arabic. For example, Urdu has contrasts between aspirated and non-aspirated consonants which are altogether unknown in Arabic. Consonantal scripts differ from most others by being written from right to left.

Syllabic scripts have one character for each syllable which exists in a particular language, i.e. there will be five separate characters to represent **ba**, **be**, **bi**, **bo** and **bu**, etc. and there need not necessarily be any resemblance of form between any or all of these. Syllabic scripts are generally designed for and applied to a single language. Very few of the world's languages are currently written in syllabic scripts.

Semi-syllabic scripts, on the other hand, are used for most of the languages of the Indian subcontinent, for many of the languages of Southeast Asia, and for Amharic and other languages of Ethiopia. Most of the characters in semi-syllabic scripts represent a sequence of a consonant and a vowel. Each set of characters sharing the same initial consonant has a similar base form with modifications indicating the particular vowel (or absence of any vowel). There are also special characters for initial vowels. The semi-syllabic scripts used for certain languages have additional modifications for tone.

BOOKS PRINTED IN THE TAMIL SEMI-SYLLABIC SCRIPT

Logographic writing systems comprise a large set of graphic signs, each of which represents a word or concept. Chinese is the best-known and most extensively used example of this. This has the advantage that all the languages of China have a common written form even though their speakers cannot communicate with each other in speech. An important disadvantage of logographic writing systems is that pupils have to spend a huge proportion of their time at school learning to read and write several thousand characters.

---

15   For a brief account of the application of these systems to previously unwritten languages, see Baker (1997). For a comprehensive description of the world's writing systems, see Daniels & Bright (1996).

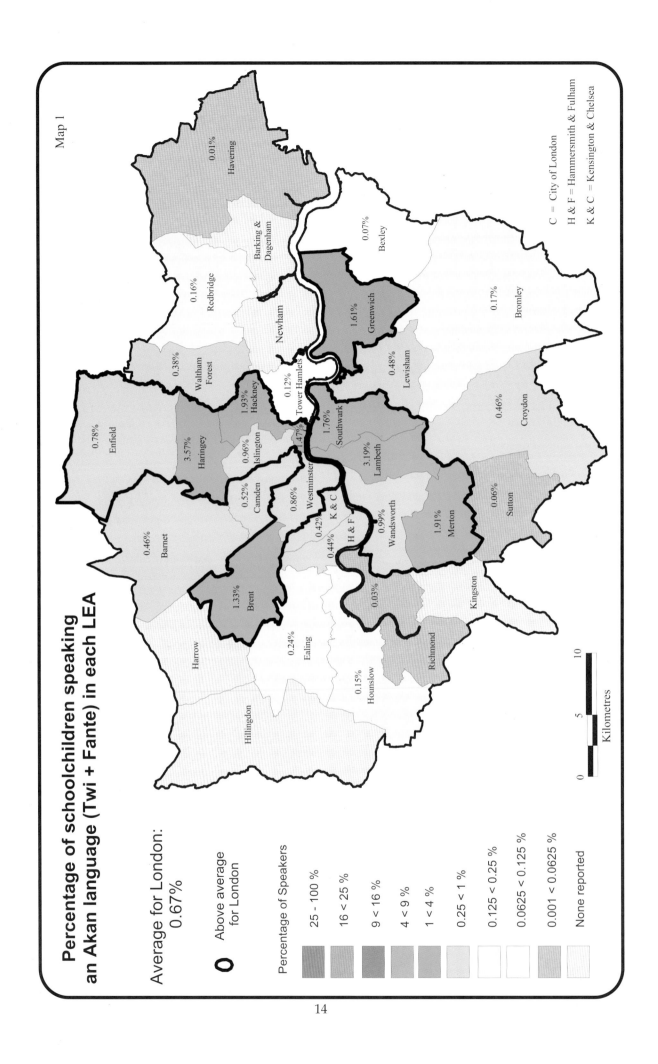

**Percentage of schoolchildren speaking
an Akan language (Twi + Fante) in each LEA**

Map 1

Average for London:
0.67%

O   Above average
    for London

Percentage of Speakers

25 - 100 %
16 < 25 %
9 < 16 %
4 < 9 %
1 < 4 %
0.25 < 1 %
0.125 < 0.25 %
0.0625 < 0.125 %
0.001 < 0.0625 %
None reported

C = City of London

H & F = Hammersmith & Fulham

K & C = Kensington & Chelsea

Havering 0.01%
Barking & Dagenham
Redbridge 0.16%
Newham 0.12%
Bexley 0.07%
Greenwich 1.61%
Bromley 0.17%
Waltham Forest 0.38%
Lewisham 0.48%
Hackney 1.93%
Tower Hamlets
Southwark 1.76%
Croydon 0.46%
Enfield 0.78%
Haringey 3.57%
Islington 0.96%
1.47%
Lambeth 3.19%
Camden 0.52%
Westminster 0.86%
K & C 0.42%
Sutton 0.06%
Barnet 0.46%
H & F 0.44%
Wandsworth 0.99%
Merton 1.91%
Brent 1.33%
0.03%
Kingston
Harrow
Ealing 0.24%
Richmond
Hillingdon
Hounslow 0.15%

0   5   10
Kilometres

14

5.3 Alphabetical list of the languages of London

Abe is an **Aframic** language of the Ivory Coast. [This survey: 3 speakers (all Lewisham)]

*Abkhaz is a language of the **Caucasus** geozone spoken in Abkhazia (Russian Federation).

Abua is a **Benuic** language spoken in Nigeria. [This survey: 3 speakers (Haringey, Islington, Lewisham].

Acholi is a **Nilotic** language spoken in Uganda and Sudan. It is closely related to Luo (Dhopaluo). [This survey: 122 speakers (Southwark;[16] 18 Lewisham)].

Adangme is an **Aframic** language spoken in Ghana which is related to Gā. [This survey: reported only in Westminster where Gā and Adangme were counted together as a single language[17]].

'Afar is a **Cushitic** language spoken in Ethiopia, Eritrea and Djibouti. [This survey: 1 speaker (Hammersmith & Fulham)].

Afrikaans derives from the **Germanic** language, Dutch, with which it remains largely mutually intelligible. It is spoken by a few million people in South Africa. [This survey: 64 speakers (22 Enfield)].

Akan (Twi+Fante). The Akan people of southern Ghana speak a number of closely related **Aframic** languages, including Fante and Twi, which are known collectively as Akan. (*Ashanti*, reported by some LEAs is a dialect of Twi.) There are several million speakers in all, accounting for about 40% of the population of Ghana. [This survey: 6,094 speakers (1,145 Haringey)].

As Map 1 (opposite) shows, the areas in which the Akan languages are spoken by an above-average proportion of children run from Enfield in the north to Merton in the south, and from Brent in the northwest to Greenwich in the south. The highest percentage – more than five times the London average – is found in Haringey and, within this borough, Map 2 (following) indicates that Akan-speakers are most numerous in the northestern (Tottenham) area of the borough. Akan is second to Turkish in Haringey (Table 5) and also occupies second place in Merton.

Akpafu is an **Aframic** language of northern Ghana. [This survey: 4 speakers (all Lewisham)].

Aku –> Krio

Albanian (Shqipe) is the only **Albanic** language and is not closely related to any other Indo-European language. [This survey: 934 speakers (182 Westminster)].

The percentage of children who speak Albanian is above the average for London in a small area from Brent and Hammersmith to Haringey (see Map 3, following). Although the proportion exceeds five times the London average in Brent, Kensington & Chelsea and West-minster, Albanian does not feature among the top three languages in any borough (Table 5).

*Alur is a **Nilotic** language spoken in Congo/Zaire and Uganda.

Ambo is a **Bantuic** language of Zambia. [This survey; 2 speakers (both Islington)].

Amharic is a **Semitic** language with official status in Ethiopia. It is written in the Ethiopic semi-syllabic script. [This survey: 431 speakers (58 Westminster)]

Map 5 (following) shows that the areas in which the highest proportion of Amharic-speaking children live are Kensington & Chelsea and Westminster with more than five times the London average.

Anaang is a **Benuic** language closely related to Ibibio, spoken in Nigeria; see *Efik+Ibibio*. [This survey: reported only in Southwark[18]].

Arabic is ranked 6th in the world with 200m first-language speakers (250m including competent second-language speakers). However, while there exists a "modern standard Arabic" language with a common standard written form from Morocco to the Persian Gulf, modern colloquial Arabic differs very considerably from one place to another, to the extent that several different but related spoken Arabic languages might be recognised. Particularly important among these are Maghrebi ("western colloquial Arabic" of Morocco, Algeria and Tunisia) and Mashriqi ("eastern colloquial Arabic", spoken from Egypt to the Persian Gulf). Nevertheless, most Arabic-speakers seem disposed to regard all varieties of Arabic as forms of one language, a view probably influenced by the existence of a common written standard form of Arabic. In any case, most LEAs do not distinguish between different varieties of Arabic so this is treated here as a single entity.

Arabic is a **Semitic** language written in its own consonantal script [This survey: 11,023 speakers (1,666 Westminster)].

Map 6 shows that Arabic speakers are located mainly in Central, West and part of North London, as well as in three boroughs south of the Thames. The percentage of speakers is more than five times the average for London as a whole in Westminster and Kensington & Chelsea. Within Westminster, Map 7 indicates that Arabic speakers account for more than a quarter of children living just to the north and east of Hyde Park as well as in an area stretching from Victoria Street to the Houses of Parliament.

Arabic occupies first place in three boroughs, as indicated in Table 5, and third place in two others.

Aramaic (Assyrian) is a **Semitic** language spoken in Palestine, Syria, Lebanon, Iran, Iraq, Turkey and Azerbaijan. (The choice between the names Assyrian and Aramaic among respondents remains to be investigated but may perhaps be related to religious affiliation.) Aramaic has long been, and continues to be, written in a number of consonantal scripts. [This survey: 263 speakers (246 Ealing)].

Armenian is the only **Armenic** language and is not closely related to any other Indo-European language. It is spoken mainly in Armenia and Azerbaijan and written in its own (non-Roman) alphabet and has about 4m speakers. [This survey: 189 speakers (83 Ealing)].

---

[16] The Southwark figures (Research and Statistics Unit 1998) include a list of 29 languages indicating the percentage of children from homes in which each of these are spoken. The list also includes a percentage for "other languages" (4.7%; this figure may itself be a misprint) with a footnote which reveals that this refers to a list of 61 languages. On average, this works out to 26 speakers of each of these, and these have been entered into the basefile. However, in many cases, 26 is more than the figure reliably reported for the same language from any other borough, it must be regarded with some caution. In such cases, Southwark is listed as having the most speakers but without any number, as here, followed by the highest reliable figure from any other borough.

[17] The 40 speakers of Gā-Adangme in Westminster are represented as speakers of Gā on Map 12.

[18] See footnote 16.

15

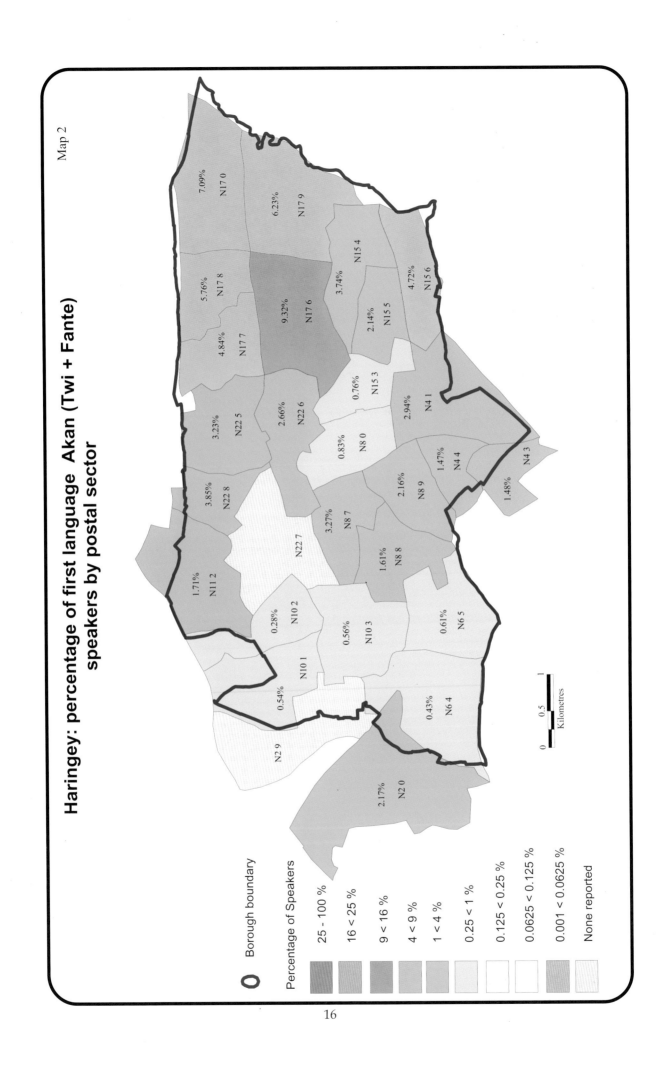

Haringey: percentage of first language Akan (Twi + Fante) speakers by postal sector

Map 2

O Borough boundary

Percentage of Speakers

- 25 - 100 %
- 16 < 25 %
- 9 < 16 %
- 4 < 9 %
- 1 < 4 %
- 0.25 < 1 %
- 0.125 < 0.25 %
- 0.0625 < 0.125 %
- 0.001 < 0.0625 %
- None reported

Kilometres
0   0.5   1

7.09% N17 0
6.23% N17 9
5.76% N17 8
4.84% N17 7
9.32% N17 6
3.74% N15 4
2.14% N15 5
4.72% N15 6
0.76% N15 3
2.94% N4 1
3.23% N22 5
2.66% N22 6
0.83% N8 0
1.48% N4 3
1.47% N4 4
2.16% N8 9
3.85% N22 8
3.27% N8 7
1.71% N11 2
1.61% N8 8
N22 7
0.28% N10 2
0.56% N10 3
0.61% N6 5
N10 1
0.54%
0.43% N6 4
N2 9
2.17% N2 0

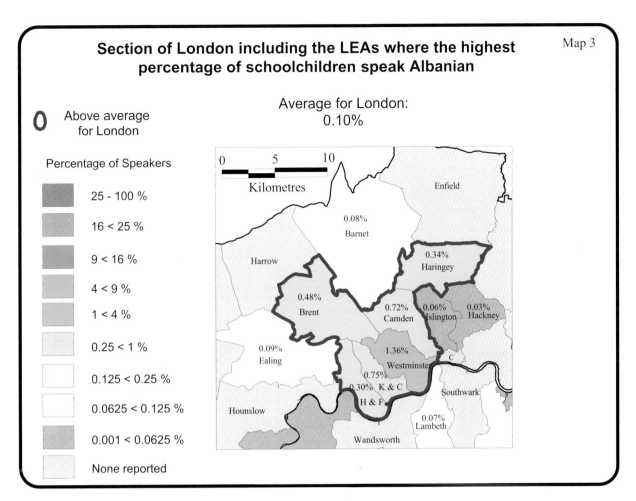

Section of London including the LEAs where the highest percentage of schoolchildren speak Albanian

Map 3

Average for London:
0.10%

O Above average for London

Percentage of Speakers

- 25 - 100 %
- 16 < 25 %
- 9 < 16 %
- 4 < 9 %
- 1 < 4 %
- 0.25 < 1 %
- 0.125 < 0.25 %
- 0.0625 < 0.125 %
- 0.001 < 0.0625 %
- None reported

0.08% Barnet

Enfield

Harrow

0.34% Haringey

0.48% Brent

0.72% Camden

0.06% Islington

0.03% Hackney

0.09% Ealing

1.36% Westminster

C

0.75% 0.30% K & C

H & F

Southwark

Hounslow

0.07% Lambeth

Wandsworth

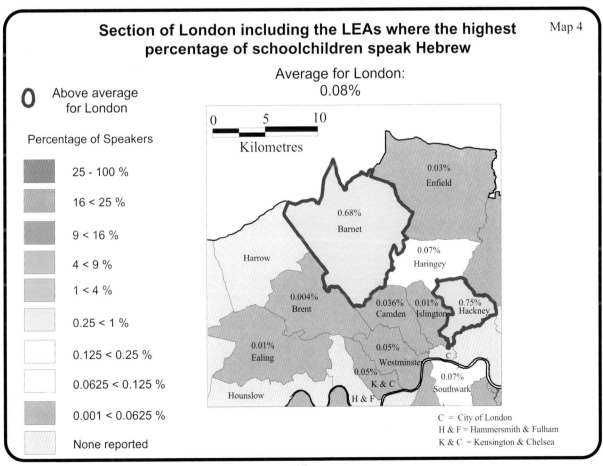

Section of London including the LEAs where the highest percentage of schoolchildren speak Hebrew

Map 4

Average for London:
0.08%

O Above average for London

Percentage of Speakers

- 25 - 100 %
- 16 < 25 %
- 9 < 16 %
- 4 < 9 %
- 1 < 4 %
- 0.25 < 1 %
- 0.125 < 0.25 %
- 0.0625 < 0.125 %
- 0.001 < 0.0625 %
- None reported

0.03% Enfield

0.68% Barnet

Harrow

0.07% Haringey

0.004% Brent

0.036% Camden

0.01% Islington

0.75% Hackney

0.01% Ealing

0.05% Westminster

C

0.05% K & C

0.07% Southwark

Hounslow

H & F

C = City of London
H & F = Hammersmith & Fulham
K & C = Kensington & Chelsea

17

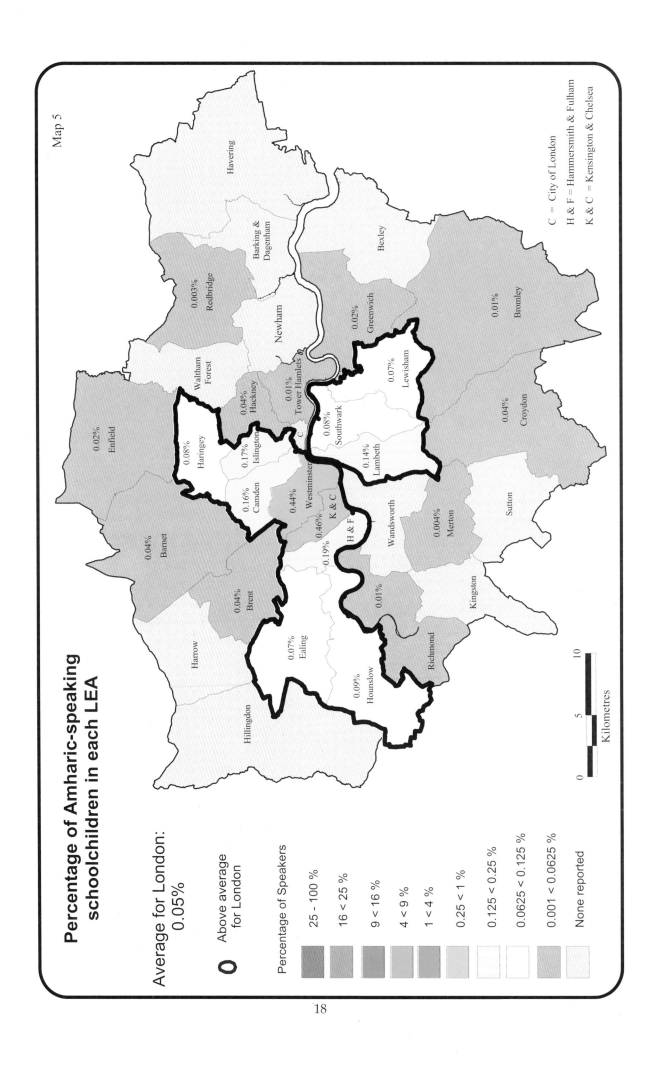

Percentage of Amharic-speaking schoolchildren in each LEA

Map 5

Average for London:
0.05%

O   Above average
     for London

Percentage of Speakers

25 - 100 %

16 < 25 %

9 < 16 %

4 < 9 %

1 < 4 %

0.25 < 1 %

0.125 < 0.25 %

0.0625 < 0.125 %

0.001 < 0.0625 %

None reported

C = City of London

H & F = Hammersmith & Fulham

K & C = Kensington & Chelsea

Havering

Barking &
Dagenham

0.003%
Redbridge

Newham

Bexley

0.02%
Greenwich

0.01%
Bromley

0.07%
Lewisham

Waltham
Forest

0.04%
Hackney

0.01%
Tower Hamlets

C

0.08%
Southwark

0.02%
Enfield

0.08%
Haringey

0.17%
Islington

0.14%
Lambeth

0.04%
Croydon

0.16%
Camden

0.44%
Westminster

0.46%
K & C

0.19%
H & F

Wandsworth

0.004%
Merton

Sutton

0.04%
Barnet

0.04%
Brent

0.01%
Richmond

Kingston

Harrow

0.07%
Ealing

0.09%
Hounslow

Hillingdon

0   5   10

Kilometres

18

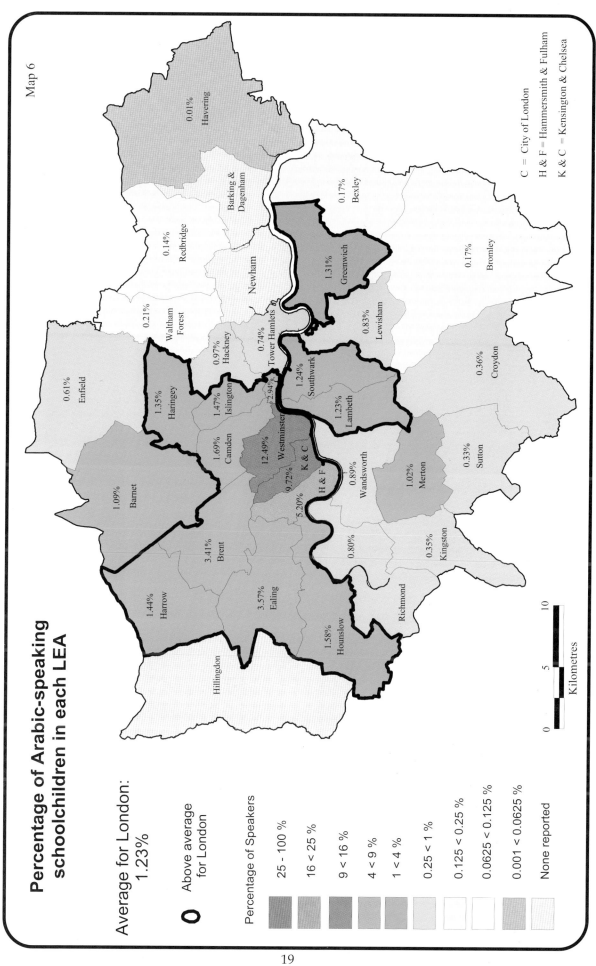

Percentage of Arabic-speaking schoolchildren in each LEA

Map 6

Average for London: 1.23%

O Above average for London

Percentage of Speakers

- 25 - 100 %
- 16 < 25 %
- 9 < 16 %
- 4 < 9 %
- 1 < 4 %
- 0.25 < 1 %
- 0.125 < 0.25 %
- 0.0625 < 0.125 %
- 0.001 < 0.0625 %
- None reported

C = City of London
H & F = Hammersmith & Fulham
K & C = Kensington & Chelsea

Havering 0.01%

Barking & Dagenham

Redbridge 0.14%

Newham

Bexley 0.17%

Greenwich 1.31%

Bromley 0.17%

Waltham Forest 0.21%

Hackney 0.97%

Tower Hamlets 0.74%

Lewisham 0.83%

Enfield 0.61%

Haringey 1.35%

Islington 1.47%

Camden 1.69%

Westminster 12.49%

K & C 9.72%

Southwark 1.24%

Lambeth 1.23%

Croydon 0.36%

Barnet 1.09%

Brent 3.41%

H & F 5.20%

Wandsworth 0.89%

Merton 1.02%

Sutton 0.33%

Harrow 1.44%

Ealing 3.57%

Hounslow 1.58%

Richmond 0.80%

Kingston 0.35%

Hillingdon

2.94%

Kilometres

0   5   10

19

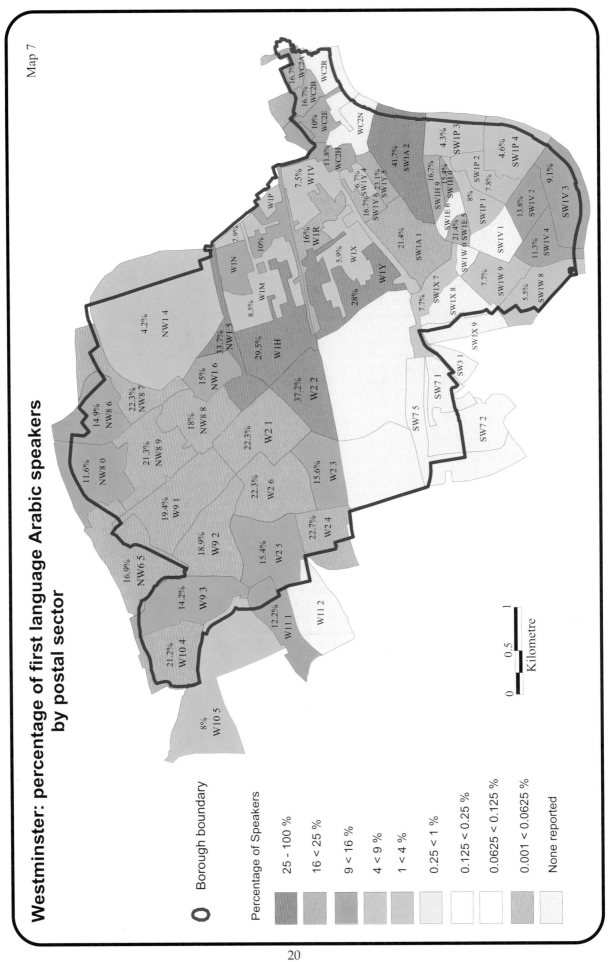

Westminster: percentage of first language Arabic speakers by postal sector

O Borough boundary

Percentage of Speakers

25 – 100 %
16 < 25 %
9 < 16 %
4 < 9 %
1 < 4 %
0.25 < 1 %
0.125 < 0.25 %
0.0625 < 0.125 %
0.001 < 0.0625 %
None reported

0   0.5   1
Kilometre

Map 7

Ashanti -> **Akan**.

Assamese is an **Indic** language spoken in the Indian state of Assam by perhaps 5m people and written in a semi-syllabic script very similar to that used for Bengali. [This survey: 1 speaker (Brent)].

Assyrian -> **Aramaic**

A-Teso *(Teso)* is a **Nilotic** language spoken in Uganda. [This survey: 14 speakers (3 each in Haringey and Lambeth)].

Azeri *(Azerbaijani)* is a language of the **Trans-Asia** geozone. It is related to Turkish and is spoken in Azerbaijan. It is currently written in an adaptation of the Cyrillic alphabet. [This survey: 2 speakers (1 each in Brent and Westminster)]

Azerbaijani -> **Azeri**

Baining is a language of the **Bismark** geozone, spoken in Papua New Guinea. [This survey: 1 speaker (Brent)].

Bajan is an abbreviation of *Barbadian*, i.e. the language of Barbados in the West Indies. The two speakers reported in this survey have been added to the figures for *English-based Creoles.*

*Bali is the name of seven different languages so cannot be correctly identified without information on the place of origin of speakers. (Bali is the name of a Tanzanian language of the **Rift-Valley** geozone, a **Hesperonesic** language spoken on the island of Bali (Indonesia), a **Manusic** language of Papua New Guinea, and four different **Bantuic** languages three of which are spoken Congo/Zaire and one in Cameroon.)

Balochi *(Baluchi)* is an **Iranic** language related to Farsi which spoken in Baluchistan (Pakistan) and written in an adaptation of the consonantal Arabic script. [This survey: 24 speakers (6 Haringey)]

Baluchi -> **Balochi**

Bantuic languages, which include Lingala, Luganda and Swahili among London's top 40 languages, all tend to have a rather similar distribution. They are mapped collectively on Map 8 (following) which shows that their speakers are clustered mainly in two areas: from Barnet to Westminster north of the Thames, and from Merton to Greenwich south of the Thames. A particular problem with the names of most Bantuic languages is that they are variably written both with and without class prefixes, e.g. Luganda is Ganda (plus the prefix lu-), Kingwana is Ngwana (with the prefix ki-), etc. While there are similarly pairs of names for almost all Bantuic languages, only variants spellings encountered in the data supplied are included in this list.

Barawan This precise name is not listed in Dalby s (1999) index. I have assumed that this relates to the *Baraawe* people of the *Brava, Swahili*-speaking area of Somalia, many of whom are now refugees.

*Bariba is a **Voltaic** language spoken in Benin and Nigeria.

Basque is the only **Euskaric** language, and is spoken in the Spanish and French Pyrenees. It is not related to any other language. [This survey: 1 speaker (Barnet)].

Bassa probably refers to the **Kruic** language of this name, spoken in Liberia. (There is also an unrelated language of the same name spoken in Nigeria by fewer people.) [This survey: 6 speakers (4 Haringey)].

*Bata is a **Mandaric** language spoken in Nigeria and Cameroon.

Beja is the only **Bejic** language and is spoken in Sudan and Eritrea. [This survey: 13 speakers (9 Lewisham)].

Belarussian is a **Slavonic** language which has official status in Belarus. [This survey: 1 speaker (Haringey)].

Bemba is a **Bantuic** language spoken in Zambia and Congo/Zaire. [This survey: 131 speakers (32 Lewisham)].

Bende is a **Bantuic** language of Tanzania. [This survey: 1 speaker (Lambeth)].

Bengali is an **Indic** language which has official status both in Bangladesh and the Indian state of West Bengal (which includes the city of Calcutta). It is written in a semi-syllabic script. There are about 250m speakers of Bengali worldwide of whom it is the primary language of about 190m. [This survey: see *Bengali+Sylheti*].

Bengali+Sylheti The great majority of school-children for whom Bengali is recorded as the home language are descendents of immigrants from Bangladesh. (Some others are from the Indian state of West Bengal.) A substantial proportion of the Bangladeshis came from Sylhet in the eastern part of that country where Sylheti, a language related to Bengali, is spoken. Many Bangladeshis in London thus speak Sylheti rather than Bengali at home. However, it is not easy to determine the proportion of speakers of Sylheti. One reason is that everyone who speaks Sylheti also knows Bengali to a greater or lesser extent and tends to regard Bengali as the cultural language of all Bangladeshis. Six boroughs record separate figures for Sylheti and Bengali, seven overtly combine Bengali and Sylheti in a single figure, and the rest record only Bengali. For these reasons, the only practical solution for this publication is to amalgamate the figures for Bengali and Sylheti as is done here. [This survey: 40,459 speakers (19,149 Tower Hamlets)]

Percentage of schoolchildren speaking a Bantuic language in each LEA

(Lingala, Luganda and Swahili are among more than 50 Bantuic languages spoken in London)

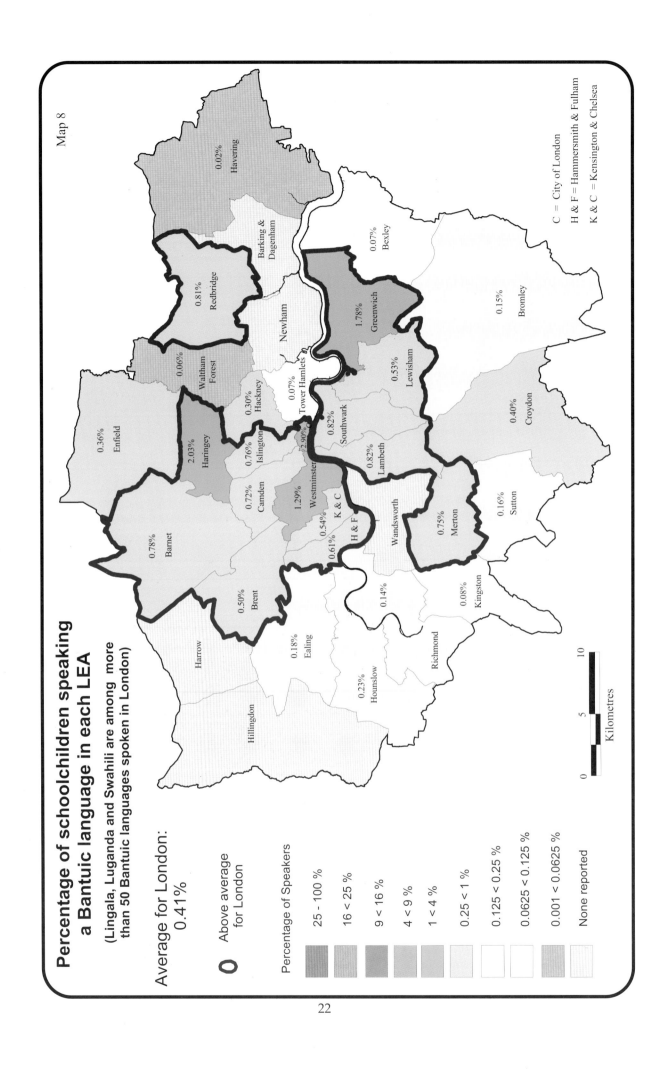

Map 8

Average for London: 0.41%

O   Above average for London

Percentage of Speakers

	25 - 100 %
	16 < 25 %
	9 < 16 %
	4 < 9 %
	1 < 4 %
	0.25 < 1 %
	0.125 < 0.25 %
	0.0625 < 0.125 %
	0.001 < 0.0625 %
	None reported

C = City of London
H & F = Hammersmith & Fulham
K & C = Kensington & Chelsea

Kilometres
0   5   10

Havering 0.02%
Barking & Dagenham
Redbridge 0.81%
Waltham Forest 0.06%
Newham 0.07%
Bexley 0.07%
Greenwich 1.78%
Tower Hamlets 0.07%
Hackney 0.30%
Lewisham 0.53%
Enfield 0.36%
Haringey 2.03%
Islington 0.76%
Westminster 2.90%
Southwark 0.82%
Lambeth 0.82%
Croydon 0.40%
Camden 0.72%
K & C 1.29%
Barnet 0.78%
H & F 0.54%
Wandsworth 0.14%
Merton 0.75%
Sutton 0.16%
Bromley 0.15%
Brent 0.50%
K & C 0.61%
Kingston 0.08%
Harrow
Ealing 0.18%
Hounslow 0.23%
Richmond
Hillingdon

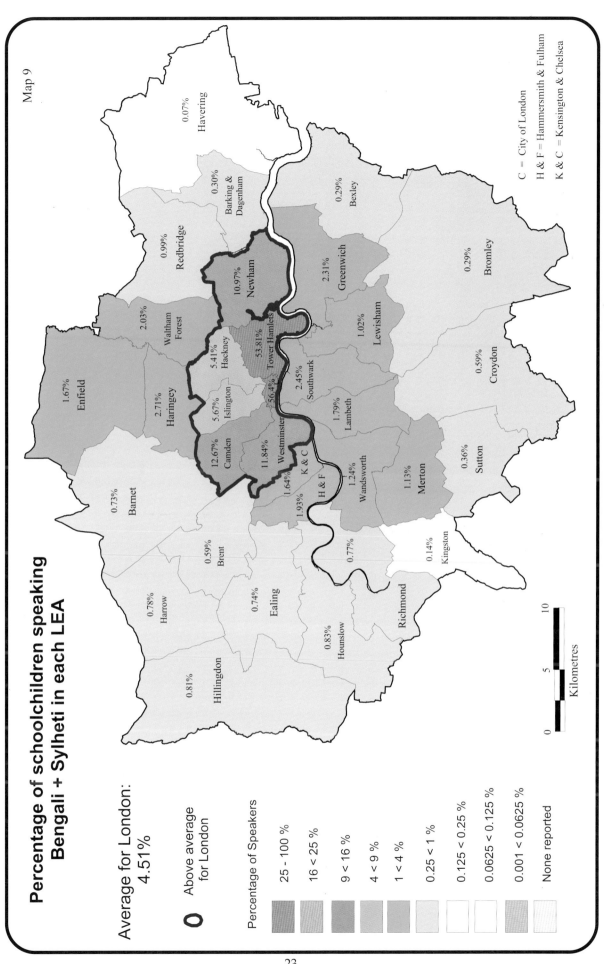

Map 9

Percentage of schoolchildren speaking Bengali + Sylheti in each LEA

Average for London: 4.51%

O   Above average for London

Percentage of Speakers

25 - 100 %
16 < 25 %
9 < 16 %
4 < 9 %
1 < 4 %
0.25 < 1 %
0.125 < 0.25 %
0.0625 < 0.125 %
0.001 < 0.0625 %
None reported

C = City of London
H & F = Hammersmith & Fulham
K & C = Kensington & Chelsea

Havering 0.07%
Barking & Dagenham 0.30%
Redbridge 0.99%
Bexley 0.29%
Newham 10.97%
Greenwich 2.31%
Waltham Forest 2.03%
Tower Hamlets 53.81%
Lewisham 1.02%
Hackney 5.41%
Bromley 0.29%
Southwark 2.45%
Enfield 1.67%
Islington 5.67%
56.4%
Lambeth 1.79%
Haringey 2.71%
Camden 12.67%
Westminster 11.84%
Croydon 0.59%
Barnet 0.73%
K & C 1.64%
Wandsworth 1.24%
Sutton 0.36%
H & F 1.93%
Merton 1.13%
Brent 0.59%
0.77%
Kingston 0.14%
Harrow 0.78%
Ealing 0.74%
Richmond
Hillingdon 0.81%
Hounslow 0.83%

0   5   10
Kilometres

23

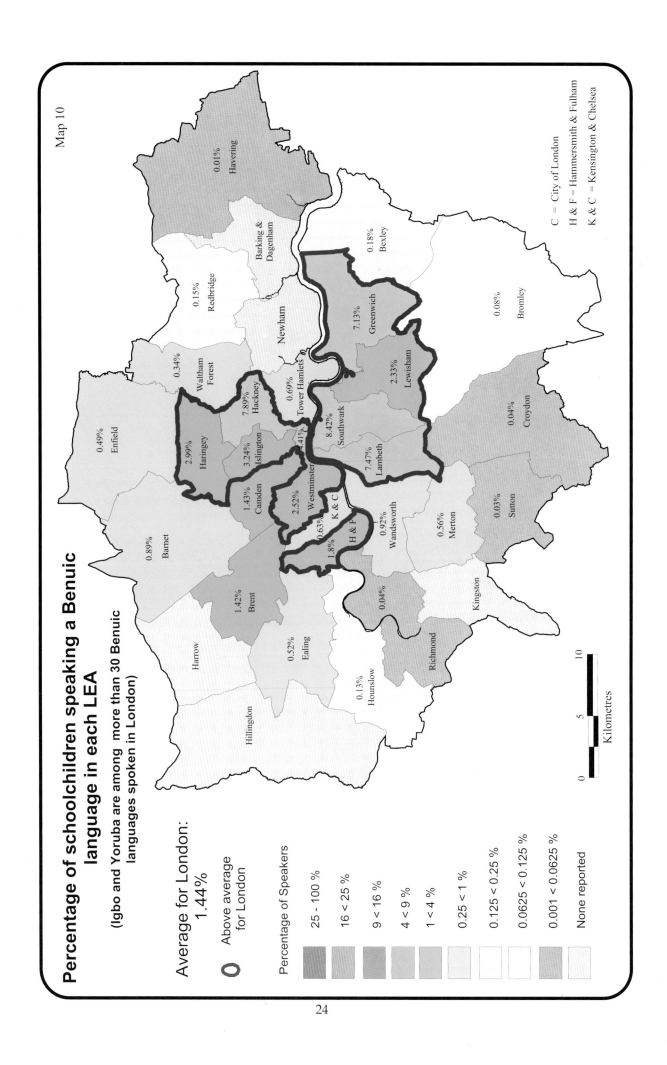

Percentage of schoolchildren speaking a Benuic language in each LEA

(Igbo and Yoruba are among more than 30 Benuic languages spoken in London)

Map 10

Average for London: 1.44%

O   Above average for London

Percentage of Speakers

	25 - 100 %
	16 < 25 %
	9 < 16 %
	4 < 9 %
	1 < 4 %
	0.25 < 1 %
	0.125 < 0.25 %
	0.0625 < 0.125 %
	0.001 < 0.0625 %
	None reported

C = City of London
H & F = Hammersmith & Fulham
K & C = Kensington & Chelsea

Kilometres
0   5   10

Havering 0.01%
Barking & Dagenham
Bexley 0.18%
Redbridge 0.15%
Newham
Greenwich 7.13%
Bromley 0.08%
Waltham Forest 0.34%
Tower Hamlets 0.69%
Lewisham 2.33%
Hackney 7.89%
Enfield 0.49%
Islington 3.24%
Haringey 2.99%
Southwark 8.42%
Croydon 0.04%
Camden 1.43%
Lambeth 7.47%
Westminster 2.52%
K & C 0.63%
Barnet 0.89%
Sutton 0.03%
H & F 1.8%
Wandsworth 0.92%
Merton 0.56%
Brent 1.42%
Ealing 0.52%
Richmond 0.04%
Kingston
Harrow
Hounslow 0.13%
Hillingdon

Although Bengali+Sylheti is the home language of more London schoolchildren than any other language (apart from English), Map 9 reveals that speakers are largely concentrated in the central area stretching from Westminster to Newham. The percentage is more than five times as great as that for London as a whole in Tower Hamlets and the adjoining City of London. The fact that the highest percentage of all is given for the City serves to emphasize the point that our figures relate only to children attending LEA schools rather than to the population as a whole. Although a great many people work in the City, its resident population is small; only one primary school is the direct responsibility of the Corporation of London just over half of whose pupils are from Bengali- or Sylheti-speaking homes.

In Table 5, Bengali+Sylheti occupies first place in five boroughs and second or third place in a further two.

Benin is a variant of *Bini*, itself an alternative name for *Edo*.

The **Benuic** languages, which include Yoruba and Igbo among London□s top 40, all show a similar distribution across London and are mapped collectively on Map 10 (opposite). The percentage of speakers is about five times the London average in Greenwich, Hackney, Lambeth and Southwark.

Berber is the collective English name for a number of different but related **Tamazic** languages which together have around 10m speakers who live mainly in Morocco and Algeria. (Speakers of Berber languages do not use the word □Berber□ themselves and this is sometimes considered a pejorative term.) Most North-African-born Berbers in London also speak Arabic which is generally accorded more status with the result that Arabic rather than Berber may have been recorded as the home language of their children in many cases. The Berber languages are often written in the Arabic script but the Tifinigh script, traditionally used for writing Tuareg, is beginning to be used for other Berber languages. [This survey: 10 speakers (4 Ealing)].

Berri is the name of a **Saharic** languages and of a **Nilotic** language, both of which are spoken in Sudan.

Bihari is an **Indic** language spoken in Bihar and adjoining areas of India by some 50m people which is written in the Devanagari semi-syllabic script.

Bimoba is a **Voltaic** language spoken in Ghana. [This survey: 1 speaker (Brent)].

Bini –> *Edo*

Bisayan (Visayan) is the name of a group of **Hesperonesic** languages (which includes Cebuano and Hiligaynon). All of these are spoken on various islands in the Philippines. [This survey (excluding Cebuano and Hiligaynon): 2 speakers (Barnet and Haringey)].

Bosnian –> *Serbian/Croatian*

Brass –> *Nembe*

Brava –> *Swahili*

British Sign Language was recorded as the language of only 7 children in this survey. The true figure for children using BSL is probably many times greater than this. It may be that many boroughs felt that only the recording of spoken languages was required.

Bukusu is a **Bantuic** language of Kenya. [This survey: 26 speakers (Southall)[19]].

Bulgarian, the official language of Bulgaria, is a **Slavonic** language written in the Cyrillic alphabet. [This survey: 248 speakers (40 Kensington & Chelsea)].

Buli is the name of three different languages so cannot be correctly identified without knowing the speakers' place of origin. (These are: a **Bauchic** language of Nigeria, a **Himayapenic** language of Indonesia, and a **Voltaic** language of Ghana.)

Buma is the name of three different languages so cannot be correctly identified without knowing the speakers' place of origin. (These are: a **Solomonic** language of the Solomon islands, a **Bantuic** language of Congo/Zaire, and a **Nilotic** language of Ethiopia.)

Burmese is an **Irrawaddic** language spoken by some 35m speakers in Burma, written in its own semi-syllabic script. [This survey: 39 speakers (15 Lewisham)].

Burushaski is the collective name for three languages of the **South-Asia** geozone spoken in Pakistan and Kashmir.

Calabari –> Kalabari

Cambodian –> Khmer

Cantonese is a **Sinitic** language ranked 19th in the world with 70m speakers. It is written in the Chinese logographic script. [This survey (part estimated – see below): 6,922 speakers (674 Southwark)].

In the past, most local education authorities recorded "Chinese" as the language spoken by all children whose ancestors came from China. Since then it has increasingly been recognised that Cantonese was a language altogether distinct from Putonghua (and other varieties). In the present survey, only five boroughs used the single term "Chinese" and for these we have estimated the numbers of Cantonese speakers.[20]

The area in which an above-average proportion of Cantonese speakers live extends from Barnet to Lambeth to Bexley. Within this area, Greenwich has more than five times the London average. It is one of the few "top 40" languages (Table 1) which is best represented in a borough located south of the Thames. Although not one of the best represented languages in Westminster, Map 11 (following) shows that most of its Cantonese speakers are, predictably, located in Soho and Covent Garden where there are a great many Chinese restaurants.

[19] See footnote 16.

[20] For all LEAs recording Cantonese and Putonghua (Mandarin) separately (and in some cases other varieties of Chinese), these figures were totalled and the average prercentage of Cantonese speakers among these was calculated. This percentage was then applied to the figure for "Chinese" in the five boroughs recording only the latter in order to obtain an estimate of the likely number of Cantonese speakers. These figures are included in the total for Cantonese and on Map 10.[19]

Westminster: percentage of first language Cantonese speakers by postal sector

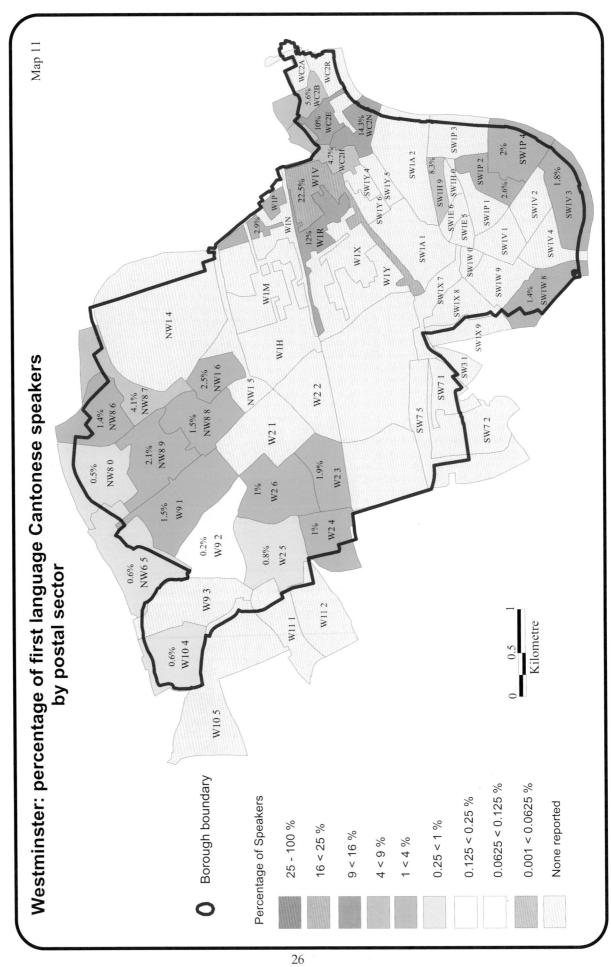

Map 11

O   Borough boundary

Percentage of Speakers

25 - 100 %
16 < 25 %
9 < 16 %
4 < 9 %
1 < 4 %
0.25 < 1 %
0.125 < 0.25 %
0.0625 < 0.125 %
0.001 < 0.0625 %
None reported

0   0.5   1
Kilometre

While Cantonese nowhere occupies first place, Table 5 shows it in second or third place in a total of four boroughs.

Carib is a **Caribic** language formerly spoken on many of the Caribbean islands and which is still spoken in parts of Venezuela, the Guianas and Brazil. In the two boroughs where this is reported, it could well be that this was used as an alternative name for Afro-Caribbean Patwa (see English-based Creoles). [This survey: 16 speakers (14 Islington)].

Catalan is a **Romanic** language with official status in Andorra. It is also spoken in southwestern France, northeast Spain, and the Balearic islands by perhaps 11m people in all. [This survey: 12 speakers (3 Kensington & Chelsea)]

Cebuano is a **Hesperonesic** language of the Philippines with some 17m speakers. It is one of the languages known collectively as Bisayan (see entry for further details). [This survey: 5 speakers (4 Barnet)].

Che is a **Benuic** language of Nigeria. [This survey: 2 speakers (both Lewisham)].

Chewa (Nyanja) is a **Bantuic** language spoken in Malawi, Zambia and Mozambique by several million people. [This survey: 50 speakers (20 Barnet)].

Chiga (Kiga) is a **Bantuic** language of Rwanda and Uganda. [This survey: 1 speaker (Brent)].

Chinese. Various languages are spoken in China, all of which share a common logographic written form (see p 12). There is thus a single written language which can legitimately be called 'Chinese' but this word cannot be applied unambiguously to any single language spoken in China. The most important languages of China are *Putonghua* (Mandarin), Wu, Yue (see *Cantonese*), Min-nan, Xiang and Hakka.

In the past, many boroughs recorded 'Chinese' for all and any of the languages of China. In the present survey, all but five boroughs distinguish Cantonese from at least one other Chinese language (see entry for *Cantonese* for further details).

Chokwe is a **Bantuic** language spoken in Angola, Congo/Zaire and Zambia. [This survey: 1 speaker (Westminster)].

Creole –> *English-based Creoles, French-based Creoles, Portuguese-based Creoles*

Croatian –> *Serbian/Croatian*

Czech is a **Slavonic** language which has official status in the Czech Republic. It is very closely related to Slovak and, if these two are treated together, the combined number of speakers is about 17m. [This survey (Czech only): 224 speakers (36 Bexley)].

*Dagari is a **Voltaic** language spoken in Ghana and Burkina Faso.

Dagbane is a **Voltaic** language of Ghana and Togo. [This survey: 6 speakers (4 Westminster)].

Damara is a **Khoisanic** language spoken in Namibia. [This survey: 1 speaker (Islington)].

Danish is a **Germanic** language with official status in Denmark. [This survey: 67 speakers (11 Ealing)].

Dari is an **Iranic** language spoken in Afghanistan which is closely related to *Farsi*, and which may well have been reported as Persian or Farsi in some boroughs. [This survey: 38 speakers (25 Ealing)].

*Dhivehi (Divehi) is an Indic language whose closest relation is Sinhala (of Sri Lanka), and which has official status in the Maldive islands. It is written in its own unique, basically consonantal script which consists mainly of characters derived from numerical symbols of both Arabic and local origin.

Dhopadhola is a **Nilotic** language of Uganda and Kenya. (Dhopadhola is closely related to one of the two languages both called Luo and Lwo and, in view of this ambiguity, it seems preferable to record Dhopadhola as a separate language.) [This survey: 1 speaker (Lambeth)]

Dinka is the name of a group of **Nilotic** languages spoken in Sudan. [This survey: 54 speakers (35 Camden)].

*Divehi –> *Dhivehi*

Dutch is a **Germanic** language with official status in the Netherlands. It is closely related to Flemish and Afrikaans. If these three languages are considered a single entity on the basis of inter-intelligibility, the combined number of speakers is about 30m. [This survey (Dutch only) 210 (Southwark;[21] 26 Barnet)].

Ebira (Igbira) is a **Benuic** language spoken in Nigeria. [This survey: 5 speakers (3 Lewisham)].

Ebo is an old, inappropriate spelling of *Igbo.*

Edo (Bini, Benin) is a **Benuic** language spoken in Nigeria. [This survey: 140 speakers (52 Southwark)].

Efik+Ibibio. Efik and Ibibio are two very closely related **Benuic** languages of Nigeria which, together with Anaang, may be considered varieties of a single language. [This survey: 238 speakers (78 Southwark)].

Efutu is an **Aframic** language spoken in Ghana. [This survey: 5 speakers (all Lambeth)].

*Eggon is a **Benuic** language spoken in Nigeria.

*Ekpeye is a **Benuic** language spoken in Nigeria.

Eleme is a **Benuic** language spoken in Nigeria. [This survey: 2 speakers (both Greenwich)].

*Emai is a **Benuic** language of Nigeria.

English is a **Germanic** language ranked 2nd in the world with 1000m speakers worldwide (of whom this is the first language of 400m). It is the majority language in the UK, USA, Canada, Australia and New Zealand. [This survey: 608,490 monolingual in English].

English-based Creoles are spoken in Jamaica, most of the East Caribbean islands from the Virgin Islands down to Trinidad, and in Guyana. Krio, spoken in Sierra Leone, is also an English-based Creole. All these languages are closely related historically (Baker 1999) and, with the partial exception of Krio, are mutually intelligible. They may thus justifiably be treated as a single language. However, the available figures for the English-based Creoles are unsatisfactory for a number of reasons:

(a) Apart from Krio, which is so spelled wherever it relates to Sierra Leone,[22] English-based Creoles are mostly recorded as Patwa (or Patois, or Patua) but this word is often preceded by Afro-Caribbean or the name of or derived from a particular territory (e.g. Jamaican Patwa). The word Creole is also sometimes used. Both

---

[21]   See footnote 16.

[22]   Many people do not realise that the name Krio derives from 'Creole' and assume this to be the name of an indigenous African language.

Patwa and Creole are potentially ambiguous in that they can be applied to both English-based and French-based Creole languages.[23]

(b) Six boroughs do not record any speakers of English-based Creoles under any of the names listed under (i): Barking & Dagenham, Bexley, Harrow, Hillingdon, Newham, and Wandsworth. A further five - Croydon, Kensington & Chelsea, Lambeth, Merton, and Richmond – acknowledge some speakers of Krio but none of any of the other names listed under (i). It is virtually certain that all eleven of these boroughs have schoolchildren from homes in which an English-based Creole is the principal language. It would appear that all such children have been counted as speakers of English.[24]

(c) At the opposite extreme of the boroughs listed under (b), Lewisham reports 29,56% of its schoolchildren as being from Afro-Caribbean Patwa-speaking homes. If this were really so, it would mean that the majority of all children from English Creole-speaking homes lived in Lewisham. The more probable explanation is that all children belonging to the Afro-Caribbean ethnic category have been recorded as speakers of Afro-Caribbean Patwa.

(d) A further complication is that, among many London schoolchildren, the word Patwa seems to be increasingly and loosely applied to what might alternatively be termed "Afro-Caribbean London English". 25 years ago, the parents of most locally-born Afro-Caribbean children spoke the English-based Creole of their place of birth. Today□s London-born Afro-Caribbean children are more likely to hear such speech from their grandparents than from their parents. What many seem to call Patwa today includes a lot of words and expressions from the Caribbean, as well as others which seem to have been adopted from Black American English, but which, in terms of grammar, appears to have much in common with the popular English of central London.

For all the above reasons, any attempt to map the distribution of English-based Creoles across London would give a very distorted picture of the reality. No such attempt is made here.

Eritrean probably refers to *Tigrinya(Tigray)* which has official status in Eritrea. However, since other languages are also spoken in Eritrea, this figure has not been added to those of Tigrinya here. [This survey: 28 speakers (15 Camden)].

Esan(Ishan) is a **Benuic** language of Nigeria. [This survey: 47 speakers (Southwark;[25] 6 Lambeth)].

Estonian is a **Uralic** language related to Finnish and is the official language of Estonia. [This survey: 8 speakers (2 Kensington & Chelsea)].

Ewe is an **Aframic** language of Togo and Ghana. [This survey: 124 speakers (Southwark;[26] 21 Haringey)].

Ewondo (Yaunde) is a **Bantuic** language spoken in Cameroon. [This survey: 7 speakers (6 Westminster)].

Fang is a **Bantuic** language spoken in Cameroon, Equatorial Guinea and Gabon. [This survey: 1 speaker (Lambeth)].

Fante –> Akan

Farsi (Persian) is an **Iranic** language with official status in Iran. It is also current in parts of Tajikistan and Afghanistan, with some 40m speakers in all. Farsi is written in an adaptation of the consonantal Arabic script. [This survey: 3,279 speakers (618 Barnet)].

The distribution of Farsi across London (Map 12, overleaf) is somewhat similar to that of Arabic (Map 5). Both languages also have their highest proportion of speakers in Westminster. However, the percentage does not quite reach five times the London average for Farsi in any borough, nor does it feature among the top three languages in any LEA (see Table 5).

Fijian is a **Transpacific** language spoken in Fiji. [This survey: 78 speakers (36 Lambeth)].

Filipino –> Tagalog

Finnish is a **Uralic** language spoken mainly in Finland. [This survey: 148 speakers (48 Lambeth)].

Flemish is a **Germanic** language with official status in Belgium and about 5m speakers. It is very closely related to *Dutch* with which it may be considered to form a single language. [This survey (Flemish only) 11 speakers (3 each in Barnet and Lewisham)].

Fon is an **Aframic** language spoken in Benin. [This survey: 2 speakers (1 each in Lambeth and Lewisham)].

Frafra –> Gurenge

French is ranked 12th in the world with 125m speakers in all of whom 90m are primary speakers. It is a **Romanic** language which has official status in France and in at least 20 other countries. [This survey: 5,609 speakers (573 Lewisham)].

The area in which there is an above-average percentage of speakers of French extends from Enfield in the north to Croydon in the south, and from Ealing to Greenwich but nowhere is the proportion as much as five times the average. In Table 5, French is ranked third in both Croydon and Lewisham.

---

23   In the West Indian islands of Dominica and St Lucia both a French-based Creole and an English-based Creole are spoken. For the purposes of Table 1 only, wherever Patwa (in any spelling) or Creole are used by themselves in data obtained from local education authorities, they are assumed to relate to English-based Creoles.

24   The view that English-based Creoles are "dialects, not languages' is one which Baker has heard expressed on several occasions as justification for recording speakers of them as speakers of English. The same applies to the French-based Creoles.

25   See footnote 16.

26   See footnote 16.

Percentage of Farsi (Persian) speaking schoolchildren in each LEA

Map 12

Average for London: 0.37%

O Above average for London

C = City of London
H & F = Hammersmith & Fulham
K & C = Kensington & Chelsea

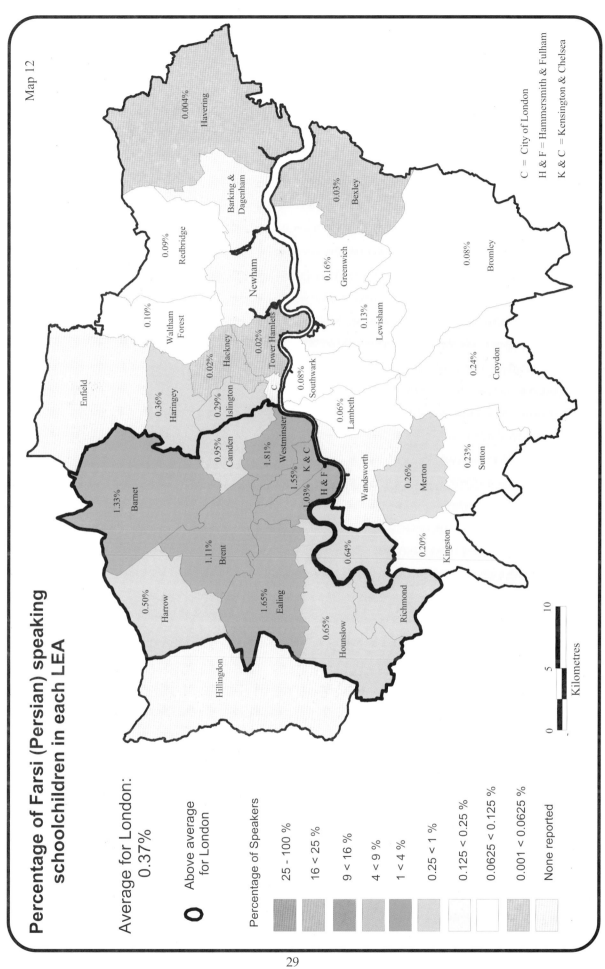

Havering 0.004%

Barking & Dagenham

Bexley 0.03%

Redbridge 0.09%

Newham

Greenwich 0.16%

Bromley 0.08%

Waltham Forest 0.10%

Hackney 0.02%

Tower Hamlets 0.02%

Lewisham 0.13%

Haringey 0.36%

Islington 0.29%

C

Southwark 0.08%

Croydon 0.24%

Enfield

Camden 0.95%

Westminster 1.81%

Lambeth 0.06%

Barnet 1.33%

K & C 1.55%

H & F 1.03%

Wandsworth

Sutton 0.23%

Brent 1.11%

Merton 0.26%

Harrow 0.50%

Ealing 1.65%

Hounslow 0.64%

Kingston 0.20%

Hillingdon

Hounslow 0.65%

Richmond

Percentage of Speakers

25 – 100 %
16 < 25 %
9 < 16 %
4 < 9 %
1 < 4 %
0.25 < 1 %
0.125 < 0.25 %
0.0625 < 0.125 %
0.001 < 0.0625 %
None reported

0   5   10
Kilometres

French-based Creoles are spoken in London by (the descendents of) immigrants from two widely-separated parts of the world – the Caribbean (mainly St Lucia and Dominica) and the Indian Ocean (Mauritius and the Seychelles). The recording of these languages in the data supplied is inferior even to that of the English-based Creoles (see above) since only 12 boroughs list these under unambiguous names (such as Creole French, Mauritian Creole, etc.).[27] In other boroughs, speakers of French-based Creoles may have been returned as 'French' or, particularly in the case of those from the West Indies, 'Patois' (which is more often applied to English-based Creoles). Those who have done research on these languages are well aware that the total of 1,664 returned from the boroughs is but a small fraction of the true number of children from homes in which a French-based Creole is spoken.[28] Due to the inadequacy of the data, no attempt has been made to map the distribution of French-based Creoles across London.

Fula (Fulani) is an **Atlantic** language spoken in more than a dozen countries from Senegal to Nigeria to southern Sudan. [This survey: 10 speakers (4 Brent)].

Fulani is the Hausa name for *Fula* (see above).

Gã (Ga, Gan) is an **Aframic** language spoken by about half a million people in the Accra area of Ghana. [This survey: 831 speakers (212 Lambeth)].

Although the area in which Gã is spoken by an above-average proportion of children is largely located in northwest London (see Map 13, following), the borough with the highest percentage of Gã speakers – in excess of five times the London average – is Lambeth.

Gaelic, recorded as the language of 291 children, is ambiguous in that it may refer to either Irish or Scottish Gaelic. (Although both written 'Gaelic', the word is pronounced "Gallic" in Scotland which may help to distinguish it from Irish Gaelic.) However, while Irish Gaelic was reported in 98 cases, there were no reports of specifically Scottish Gaelic. Both Irish and Scottish Gaelic are **Celtic** languages. [This survey: 389 (291 + 98) speakers (158 Ealing)].

Galla –> Oromo

Gan –> Gã

Ganda –> Luganda

Georgian is a language of the **Caucasus** geozone with official status in the Georgian Republic and 5m speakers. It is written in its own alphabetic script. [This survey: 14 speakers (4 each in Hammersmith & Fulham and Haringey)].

German is a **Germanic** language and is ranked 11th in the world with 125m speakers (of whom this is the first language of 100m, mainly in Germany, Austria and Switzerland). [This survey: 817 speakers (89 Barnet)].

German is spoken by an above-average percentage in much of northwest London, in Richmond, and in four South London boroughs from Lambeth to Greenwich. The highest percentage is found in Richmond where a German-language school is located. German is not among the top three languages in any London borough.

Gikuyu (Kikuyu) is a **Bantuic** language of Kenya. [This survey: 116 speakers (24 Barnet)].

Goan(ese) –> Konkani

Gogo is a **Bantuic** language of Tanzania. [This survey: 2 speakers (both Lewisham)].

Gokana is a **Benuic** language of Nigeria. [This survey: 15 speakers (12 Lewisham)].

Gola is a **Melic** language spoken in Sierra Leone and Liberia. [This survey: 2 speakers (Islington)].

*Gonja is an **Aframic** language spoken in Ghana.

Gora is a **Benuic** language spoken in Nigeria. [This survey: 2 speakers (both Barnet).

Greek is the only **Hellenic** language. It has about 12m speakers and its own alphabetic script. [This survey: 6,347 speakers (1,932 Enfield)]

Greek is spoken by an above-average proportion of children in a contiguous area of north and northwest London (see Map 14). The greatest proportion of speakers is in Enfield where the percentage is well over five times the average for London as a whole. However, Greek is second to Turkish in Enfield (see Table 5), second to Gujarati in Barnet, and occupies third place in Islington.

Gujarati is an **Indic** language spoken in the Indian state of Gujarat. In world terms, it ranks 27th with some 45m speakers. Gujarati has its own semi-syllabic script. [This survey: 26,761 speakers (5,426 Brent)].

There are two zones in which Gujarati has an above-average percentage of speakers (see Map 15, following): a western zone from Hounslow to Barnet and including both Brent and Harrow where the percentage of speakers is more than five times as great as the average for London as a whole, and a smaller eastern zone comprising Newham and Lewisham. Gujarati is the language with the largest number of speakers (other than English) in four boroughs, as shown in Table 5, and occupies second or third place in ten other boroughs.

Gurenge(Frafra) is a **Voltaic** language spoken on the border of Ghana and Burkina Faso. [This survey: 1 speaker (Lambeth)].

Gurma is a **Voltaic** language of Burkina Faso, Niger, Togo and Benin. [This survey: 4 speakers (2 Camden)].

Hahon is a **Solomonic** language spoken in Papua New Guinea. [This survey: 1 speaker (Brent)].

Hakka is a **Sinitic** language with 35m speakers, mainly in China. It is written in the Chinese logographic script. [This survey: 6 speakers (3 Westminster)].

---

27   In Islington, which is known to have quite a sizable French-based Creole-speaking community, a combined figure is given for 'French and Creole French'. In this particular case, the figure has been divided equally between French and Creole French.

28   Baker has personally carried out research on Mauritians and their language for many years and would estimate the number of people of Mauritian descent in London to be ca. 50 000 (adults as well as children). The numbers from a French Creole-speaking background in Dominica or St Lucia are fewer but still considerable.

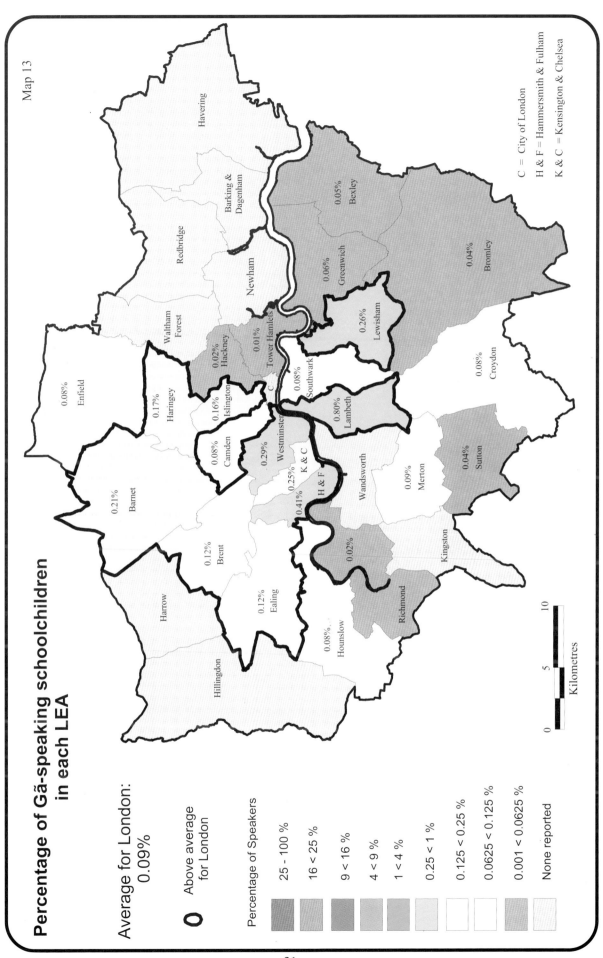

Map 13

Percentage of Gã-speaking schoolchildren in each LEA

Average for London:
0.09%

O Above average
   for London

Percentage of Speakers

	25 - 100 %
	16 < 25 %
	9 < 16 %
	4 < 9 %
	1 < 4 %
	0.25 < 1 %
	0.125 < 0.25 %
	0.0625 < 0.125 %
	0.001 < 0.0625 %
	None reported

C = City of London
H & F = Hammersmith & Fulham
K & C = Kensington & Chelsea

Kilometres
0   5   10

Havering

Barking &
Dagenham

Redbridge

Newham

0.05%
Bexley

0.06%
Greenwich

0.04%
Bromley

0.26%
Lewisham

Waltham
Forest

0.02%
Hackney

0.01%
Tower Hamlets

0.08%
Southwark

0.08%
Croydon

0.08%
Enfield

0.17%
Haringey

0.16%
Islington

0.80%
Lambeth

C

0.08%
Camden

0.29%
Westminster

0.25%
K & C

0.41%
H & F

Wandsworth

0.04%
Sutton

0.21%
Barnet

0.09%
Merton

0.12%
Brent

0.02%
Richmond

Kingston

Harrow

0.12%
Ealing

0.08%...
Hounslow

Hillingdon

31

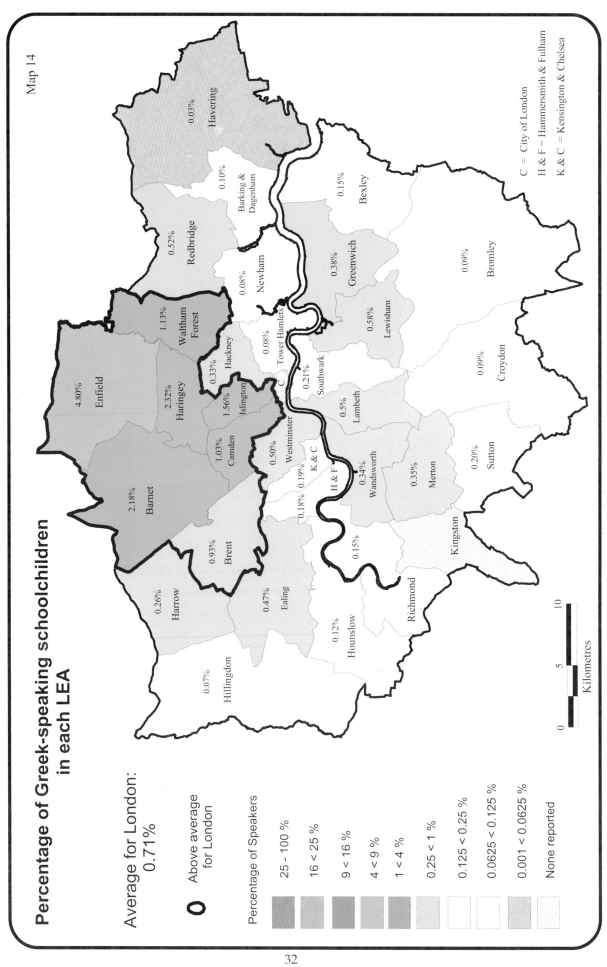

Percentage of Greek-speaking schoolchildren in each LEA

Map 14

Average for London:
0.71%

O   Above average
for London

Percentage of Speakers

	25 - 100 %
	16 < 25 %
	9 < 16 %
	4 < 9 %
	1 < 4 %
	0.25 < 1 %
	0.125 < 0.25 %
	0.0625 < 0.125 %
	0.001 < 0.0625 %
	None reported

C = City of London

H & F = Hammersmith & Fulham

K & C = Kensington & Chelsea

Hillingdon 0.07%

Harrow 0.26%

Havering 0.03%

Barking & Dagenham 0.10%

Redbridge 0.52%

Enfield 4.80%

Barnet 2.18%

Brent 0.93%

Waltham Forest 1.13%

Haringey 2.32%

Newham 0.08%

Camden 1.03%

Hackney 0.33%

Islington 1.56%

Ealing 0.47%

Westminster 0.50%

Tower Hamlets 0.08%

K & C 0.19%

H & F 0.18%

C

Southwark 0.21%

Greenwich 0.38%

Bexley 0.15%

Hounslow 0.12%

Lambeth 0.5%

Wandsworth 0.34%

Lewisham 0.58%

Richmond 0.15%

Merton 0.35%

Croydon 0.09%

Bromley 0.09%

Kingston

Sutton 0.20%

Kilometres

0   5   10

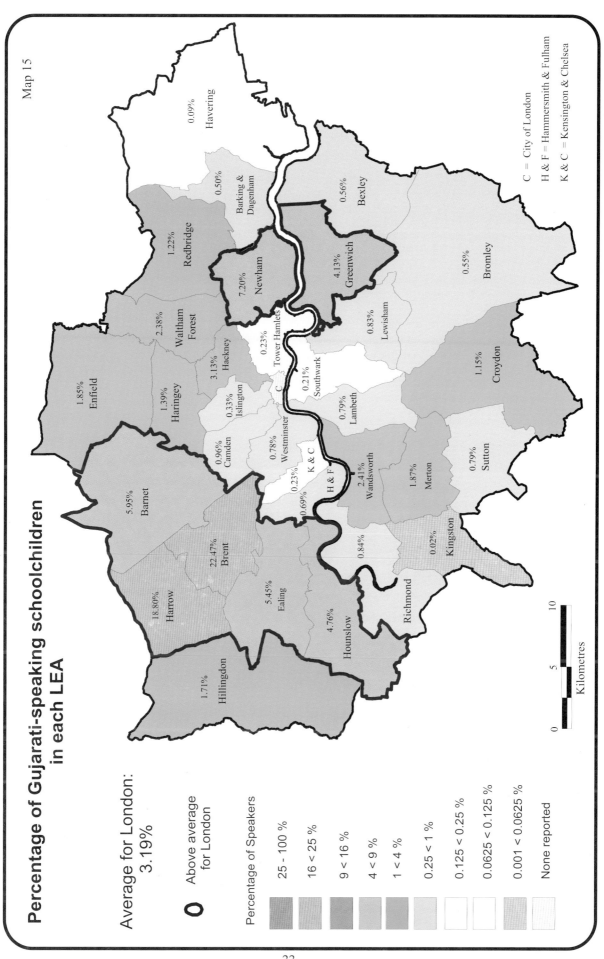

Percentage of Gujarati-speaking schoolchildren in each LEA

Average for London: 3.19%

○ Above average for London

Map 15

Percentage of Speakers

- 25 - 100 %
- 16 < 25 %
- 9 < 16 %
- 4 < 9 %
- 1 < 4 %
- 0.25 < 1 %
- 0.125 < 0.25 %
- 0.0625 < 0.125 %
- 0.001 < 0.0625 %
- None reported

C = City of London
H & F = Hammersmith & Fulham
K & C = Kensington & Chelsea

Kilometres
0   5   10

0.09% Havering
0.50% Barking & Dagenham
1.22% Redbridge
7.20% Newham
0.56% Bexley
4.13% Greenwich
0.55% Bromley
0.83% Lewisham
0.23% Tower Hamlets
2.38% Waltham Forest
3.13% Hackney
1.85% Enfield
1.39% Haringey
0.33% Islington
0.21% Southwark
1.15% Croydon
0.96% Camden
0.78% Westminster
0.79% Lambeth
5.95% Barnet
0.23% K & C
0.69% H & F
2.41% Wandsworth
1.87% Merton
0.79% Sutton
22.47% Brent
0.84% Richmond
0.02% Kingston
18.80% Harrow
5.45% Ealing
4.76% Hounslow
1.71% Hillingdon

Harari is a **Semitic** language spoken in and near Harar in Ethiopia. [This survey: 2 speakers (Camden)].

Hausa is a **Bauhic** language spoken mainly in northern Nigeria (but also in Niger, Ghana, Benin, Cameroon, Chad and Sudan). [This survey: 242 speakers (94 Ealing)].

Map 16 (following) shows that there are two areas in which an above-average percentage speak Hausa, one in the northwest and one in the southeast.

Hawaiian is a **Trans-Pacific** language spoken in Hawaii. [This survey: 1 speaker (Ealing)].

Hebrew is a **Semitic** language with official status in Israel. It is written in its own consonantal script. Map 4 (see p 17) shows the two boroughs, Barnet and Hackney, in which the proportion of Hebrew speakers exceeds five times the average for London. [This survey: 660 speakers (318 Barnet)].

Herero is a **Bantuic** language of Namibia (and parts of Angola and Botswana). [This survey: 2 (1 each in Barnet and Islington)].

The **Hesperonesic** languages, spoken mainly in Malaysia, Indonesia and the Philippines, include Tagalog among London's top 40 languages. Since the distribution of the various Hesperonesic languages across London is very similar, they are mapped collectively on Map 17 (following). There is more than five times the London average percentage for these languages in Kensington & Chelsea and Westminster.

Hiligaynon (Ilonggo) is a Hesperonesic language of the Philippines. [This survey 2 (Lewisham)].

*Hindi –> **Hindi/Urdu***

Hindi/Urdu is considered to be a single **Indic** language in this survey because Hindi and Urdu, spoken in India and Pakistan, are virtually indistinguishable in ordinary conversation and share the same basic vocabulary and grammar. People tend to regard Hindi and Urdu as separate languages because they are written in different scripts. Hindi is written in the Devanagari script while Urdu is written in an adaptation of the Arabic script.[29] Hindi/Urdu has some 900m speakers of whom this is the first language of about 550 m. [This survey: 26,122 speakers (5,635 Newham)].[30]

While it must be acknowledged that every LEA records separate figures for Hindi and Urdu, their geographical distribution across London is very similar and this is an additional reason for treating them as a single spoken language. That said, it should be added that the number of children recorded for Urdu was almost ten times as many as that for Hindi.

As Map 18 (following) shows, Hindi/Urdu is unusual among the languages of London in that there are four areas in which it has an above-average number of speakers. It is also unusual among the "top 40" languages (Table 1) in that there is no borough in which the percentage of speakers is as much as five times as great as its average for London as a whole. The borough with the highest density of speakers is Ealing.

Table 5 shows Hindi/Urdu in first place in five boroughs, in second place in eleven, and in third place in one other.

*Hokkien –> **Min-nan***

Hungarian is a **Uralic** language with official status in Hungary. It is also spoken by minorities in neighbouring states and there are about 15m speakers in all. [This survey: 384 speakers (145 Harrow)].

Harrow is the only borough in which the percentage of Hungarian speakers is greater than five times the London average.

*Ibibio –> **Efik/Ibibio***

Ibo is a common but inaccurate spelling of *Igbo*.

Icelandic is a **Germanic** language with official status in Iceland. It is related to Norwegian and other Scandinavian languages. [This survey: 14 speakers (3 Islington)].

Idoma is a **Benuic** language of Nigeria. [This survey: 32 speakers (Southwark;[31] 3 Haringey)].

*Idon is a **Benuic** language of Nigeria.

Igala is a **Benuic** language of Nigeria. It is closely related to *Yoruba*. [This survey: 5 speakers (all Ealing)].

*Igbira –> **Ebira***

Igbo is a **Benuic** language of Nigeria spoken by some 19m people. The distribution of the Benuic languages collectively is shown on Map 10. Igbo differs from the general Benuic picture only in having its highest proportion of speakers in Lewisham (more than five times its average for London as a whole) and in being poorly represented in neighbouring Southwark. Igbo does not feature in Table 5 among the top three languages in any London borough. [This survey: 1,993 speakers (343 Lewisham)].

---

29 Literature written in Hindi and Urdu, respectively, is further distinguished by the fact that the former draws on Sanskrit for new terms whereas the latter makes extensive use of Arabic and Persian vocabulary.

30 As indicated above, provisional figures supplied by Newham appear to be somewhat exaggerated so this figure should be treated with caution.

31 See footnote 16.

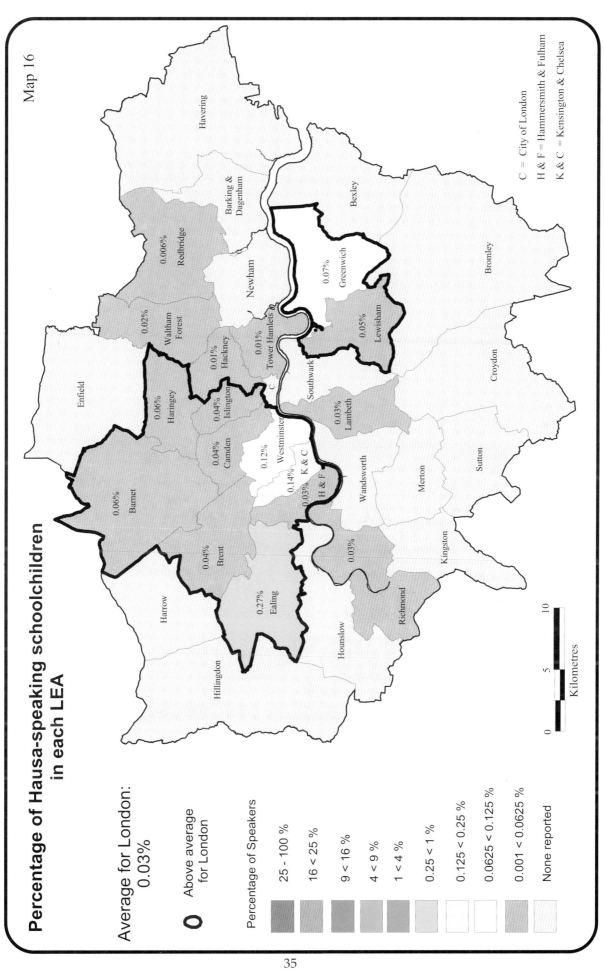

Percentage of Hausa-speaking schoolchildren in each LEA

Average for London:
0.03%

O Above average for London

Percentage of Speakers

25 - 100 %

16 < 25 %

9 < 16 %

4 < 9 %

1 < 4 %

0.25 < 1 %

0.125 < 0.25 %

0.0625 < 0.125 %

0.001 < 0.0625 %

None reported

Map 16

C = City of London
H & F = Hammersmith & Fulham
K & C = Kensington & Chelsea

Havering

Barking & Dagenham

Redbridge 0.006%

Bexley

Waltham Forest 0.02%

Newham

Greenwich 0.07%

Enfield

Hackney 0.01%

Tower Hamlets 0.01%

Lewisham 0.05%

Haringey 0.06%

Islington 0.04%

C

Southwark

Bromley

Camden 0.04%

Westminster 0.12%

Lambeth 0.03%

Croydon

Barnet 0.06%

K & C 0.14%

H & F 0.03% 0.03%

Wandsworth

Merton

Sutton

Brent 0.04%

0.03%

Kingston

Harrow

Ealing 0.27%

Richmond 0.03%

Hounslow

Hillingdon

0   5   10
Kilometres

35

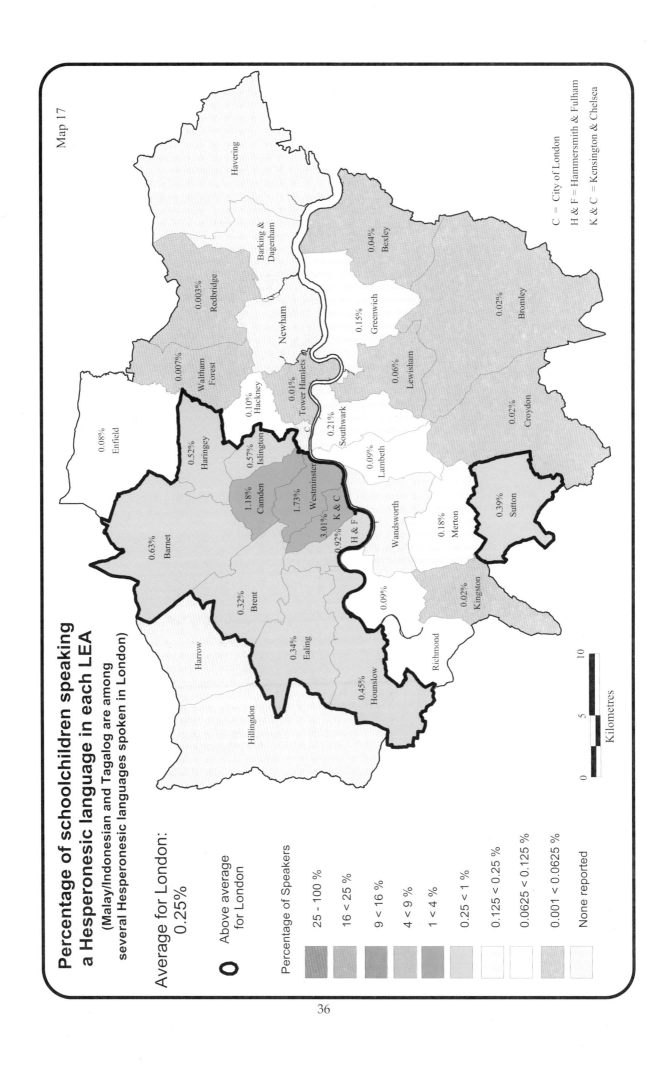

Percentage of schoolchildren speaking a Hesperonesic language in each LEA

(Malay/Indonesian and Tagalog are among several Hesperonesic languages spoken in London)

Average for London: 0.25%

O Above average for London

Percentage of Speakers

25 - 100 %
16 < 25 %
9 < 16 %
4 < 9 %
1 < 4 %
0.25 < 1 %
0.125 < 0.25 %
0.0625 < 0.125 %
0.001 < 0.0625 %
None reported

C = City of London
H & F = Hammersmith & Fulham
K & C = Kensington & Chelsea

Map 17

Kilometres
0   5   10

Havering
Barking & Dagenham
Bexley 0.04%
Bromley 0.02%
Redbridge 0.003%
Newham
Greenwich 0.15%
Lewisham 0.06%
Croydon 0.02%
Waltham Forest 0.007%
Hackney 0.10%
Tower Hamlets 0.01%
C
Southwark 0.21%
Enfield 0.08%
Haringey 0.52%
Islington 0.57%
Camden 1.18%
Westminster 1.73%
K & C 3.01%
H & F 0.92%
Lambeth 0.09%
Wandsworth 0.09%
Merton 0.18%
Sutton 0.39%
Barnet 0.63%
Brent 0.32%
Ealing 0.34%
Hounslow 0.45%
Kingston 0.02%
Richmond 0.09%
Harrow
Hillingdon

36

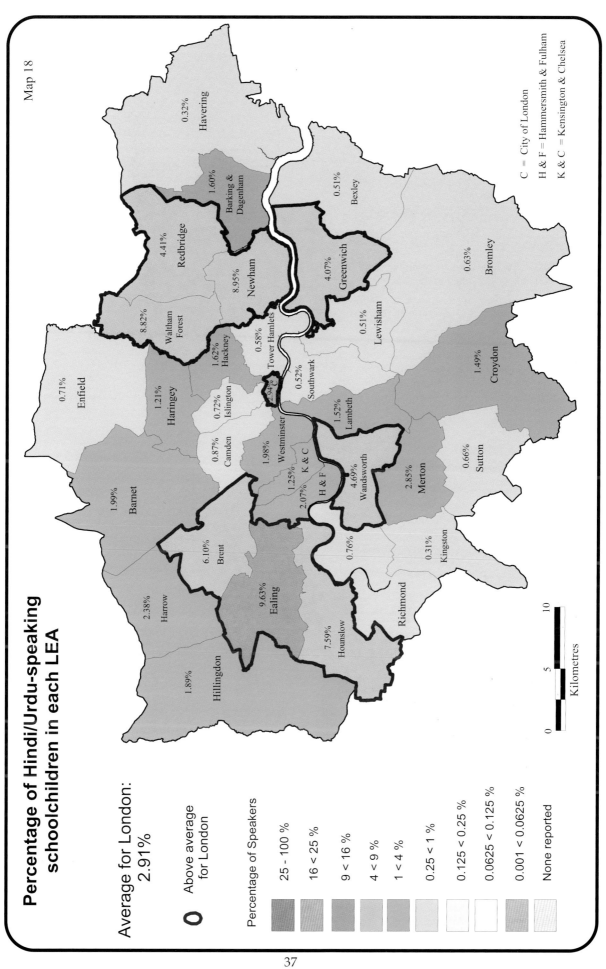

Percentage of Hindi/Urdu-speaking schoolchildren in each LEA

Map 18

Average for London: 2.91%

O — Above average for London

Percentage of Speakers

	25 - 100 %
	16 < 25 %
	9 < 16 %
	4 < 9 %
	1 < 4 %
	0.25 < 1 %
	0.125 < 0.25 %
	0.0625 < 0.125 %
	0.001 < 0.0625 %
	None reported

C = City of London
H & F = Hammersmith & Fulham
K & C = Kensington & Chelsea

0.32% Havering

1.60% Barking & Dagenham

4.41% Redbridge

8.95% Newham

0.51% Bexley

4.07% Greenwich

0.63% Bromley

8.82% Waltham Forest

1.62% Hackney

0.58% Tower Hamlets

0.51% Lewisham

0.71% Enfield

1.21% Haringey

0.72% Islington

2.94% Westminster

0.52% Southwark

1.49% Croydon

0.87% Camden

1.98% K & C

1.25% H & F

2.07%

1.52% Lambeth

1.99% Barnet

6.10% Brent

4.69% Wandsworth

2.85% Merton

0.66% Sutton

2.38% Harrow

9.63% Ealing

0.76%

0.31% Kingston

1.89% Hillingdon

7.59% Hounslow

Richmond

0 5 10

Kilometres

37

Igede is a **Benuic** language of Nigeria. [This survey: 9 speakers (4 Kensington & Chelsea)].

Ijaw is an old-fashioned spelling of **Ijo**.

Ijo is a **Deltic** language of Nigeria. [This survey: 33 speakers (9 Lewisham)].

Ikwere is a **Benuic** language of Nigeria, closely related to *Igbo*. [This survey: Southwark only[32]].

Ilocano is a **Hesperonesic** language spoken in the Philippine (Luzon island). [This survey: 32 speakers (10 Kensington & Chelsea)].

Ilonggo –> **Hiligaynon**

Indonesian –> **Malay/Indonesian**

Irish (Gaelic) –> **Gaelic**

Ishan–> Esan

Isoko is a **Benuic** language spoken Nigeria. [This survey: 3 speakers (2 Lewisham)].

Italian is a **Romanic** language which has official status in Italy and about 70m speakers in all. [This survey: 2,501 speakers (297 Barnet)].

The area in which the proportion of Italian speakers is above average stretches right across London from north to south (Map 19, following). Even so, the percentage is less than 1% throughout this area and nowhere reaches five times the average for London. It is also not among the top three languages in any borough (see Table 5), the highest figure being that for Kensington & Chelsea.

Itigo is a **Transirianic** language of Indonesia (Irian Jaya).[33] [This survey: 2 speakers (Lambeth)].

---

[32]   See footnote 16.

[33]   Since Irian Jaya seems an unlikely source of a language spoken in London, it is not impossible that Itigo may yet turn out to be an alternative name for some other language.

Itsekiri, a **Benuic** language of Nigeria, is closely related to Yoruba and is sometimes considered a variety of the latter. [This survey: 6 speakers (3 Islington)].

Jaina is recorded as the language of 7 children in Ealing. However, this word means 'follower of the Jain religion' and, since there is no language exclusively associated with this sect, this response provides no indication of what these children speak.

Japanese is a language of the **East-Asia** geozone ranked 10th in the world with 130m speakers (and the first language of 120m) and is the official language of Japan. It is written in (combinations of) several different scripts of which the most important are kanji (logographic), hiragana and katakana (both syllabic). These three scripts use characters derived from Chinese logographs. [This survey: 793 speakers (299 Barnet)].

Map 20a (following) shows an above-average proportion of Japanese speakers in several boroughs in northwest, west and southwest London. The percentage exceeds five times the average in Barnet and the City, and in Table 5 occupies third place in the latter.

Jingpho is a **Kachinic** language spoken in Burma, China (Yunnan) and India (Assam). [This survey: 1 speaker (Barnet)].

Jonkha is a **Tibetic** language which has official status in Bhutan. [This survey 1 speaker (Barnet)].

Kachchhi (Kutchi) is an **Indic** language spoken in the Rann of Kachchh [sic] in the Indian state of Gujerat which is related to *Sindhi*. It is written in the Gujarati semi-syllabic script. [This survey: 341 speakers (99 Harrow)].

Kahe is a **Bantuic** language spoken in Tanzania. [This survey: 1 speaker (Enfield)].

Kaje is a **Benuic** language spoken in Nigeria. [This survey 2 speakers (Tower Hamlets and Lambeth)].

Kakwa is a **Nilotic** language spoken in Sudan, Congo/Zaire and Uganda. [This survey: 1 speaker (Haringey)].

Kalabari (Calabari) is a **Deltic** language spoken in Nigeria. [This survey: 17 speakers (11 Lambeth)].

*Kamba refers to a **Bantuic** language of Kenya.

*Kannada is a **Dravidic** language of India.

*Karen is a collective name for the **Karenic** languages spoken in Burma and Thailand.

Kashmiri is an **Indic** language spoken in Kashmir. It is generally written in an adaptation of the Arabic consonantal script. [This survey: 6 speakers (2 Ealing)].

Katab is a **Benuic** language spoken in Nigeria. [This survey: 1 speaker (Hammersmith & Fulham)].

Kawa –> **Wa**

Kazakh is a language of the **Trans-Asia** geozone spoken mainly in Kazakhstan. It is currently written in the Cyrillic alphabet. [This survey: 1 speaker (Westminster)].

*Khana is a **Benuic** language spoken in Nigeria.

*Khasi is a language of the **South-Asia** geozone spoken in India and Bangladesh.

Khmer (Cambodian) is a language of the **South-Asia** geozone which is spoken in Cambodia. It is written in its own semi-syllabic script. [This survey: 7 speakers (2 in Barnet, 2 in Kensington & Chelsea)].

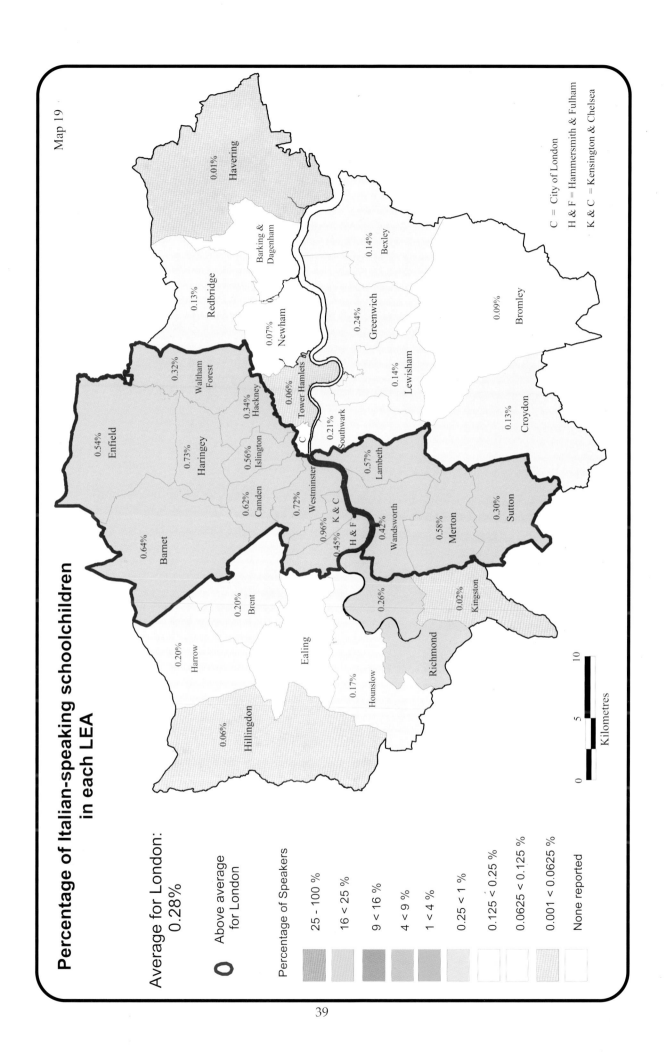

Percentage of Italian-speaking schoolchildren in each LEA

Map 19

Average for London: 0.28%

O Above average for London

Percentage of Speakers

25 - 100 %
16 < 25 %
9 < 16 %
4 < 9 %
1 < 4 %
0.25 < 1 %
0.125 < 0.25 %
0.0625 < 0.125 %
0.001 < 0.0625 %
None reported

C = City of London
H & F = Hammersmith & Fulham
K & C = Kensington & Chelsea

Havering 0.01%
Barking & Dagenham
Redbridge 0.13%
Newham 0.07%
Bexley 0.14%
Greenwich 0.24%
Bromley 0.09%
Lewisham 0.14%
Waltham Forest 0.32%
Hackney 0.34%
Tower Hamlets 0.06%
C
Southwark 0.21%
Croydon 0.13%
Enfield 0.54%
Haringey 0.73%
Islington 0.56%
Camden 0.62%
Westminster 0.72%
Lambeth 0.57%
Barnet 0.64%
K & C 0.96%
H & F 0.45%
Wandsworth 0.42%
Merton 0.58%
Sutton 0.30%
Brent 0.20%
Harrow 0.20%
Ealing
Kingston 0.02%
Hounslow 0.17%
Richmond 0.26%
Hillingdon 0.06%

0   5   10
Kilometres

39

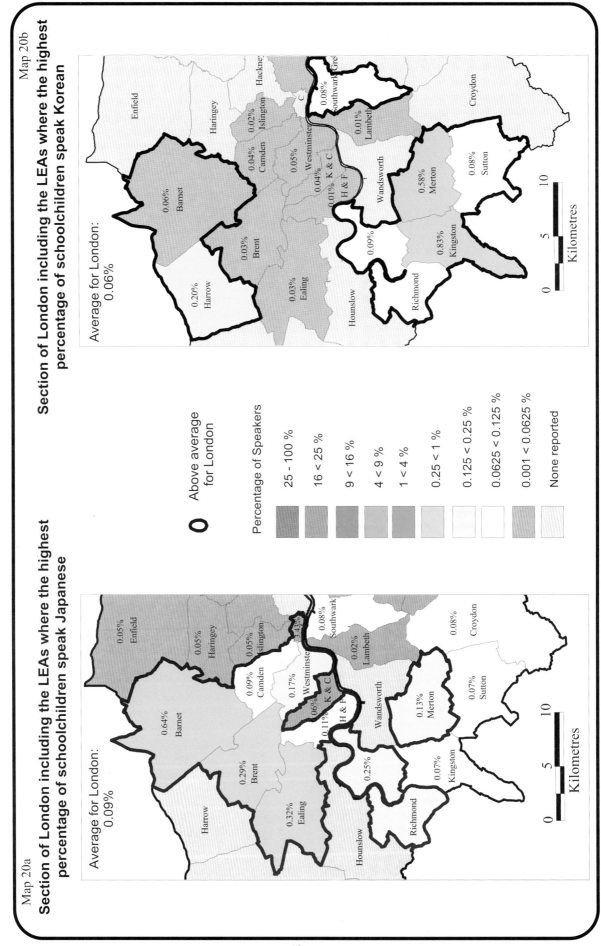

Map 20b

Section of London including the LEAs where the highest percentage of schoolchildren speak Korean

Average for London:
0.06%

Map 20a

Section of London including the LEAs where the highest percentage of schoolchildren speak Japanese

Average for London:
0.09%

Above average
for London

Percentage of Speakers

25 - 100 %

16 < 25 %

9 < 16 %

4 < 9 %

1 < 4 %

0.25 < 1 %

0.125 < 0.25 %

0.0625 < 0.125 %

0.001 < 0.0625 %

None reported

40

Ki probably refers to the **Benuic** language of this name spoken in Nigeria and Cameroon. (It might alternatively refer to a Bantuic language, Ki, also known as Ngoro, spoken in Cameroon.) [This survey: 11 speakers (all Greenwich)].

Kiga > Chiga

Kikuyu –> Gikuyu

Kimeru is a **Bantuic** language spoken in Kenya.

Kingwana (Ngwana) is a **Bantuic** language of Congo/Zaire which is very closely related to Swahili and is often considered a variety of the latter. [This survey: 2 speakers (Lewisham)].

Kirghiz is a language of the **Trans-Asia** geozone spoken in Kirghiztan. It is currently written in the Cyrillic alphabet. [This survey: 2 speakers (Kingston)].

Kirundi (Rundi) is a **Bantuic** language with official status in Burundi. [This survey: 31 speakers (Southwark;[34] 2 each in Haringey and Hammersmith & Fulham)].

Kisi is a **Melic** language of Sierra Leone, Guinea and Liberia. [This survey: 1 speaker (Barnet)].

Komi may refer either to a **Uralic** language spoken in the Russian Federation or to a Bantuic language of the same name spoken in Gabon. [This survey: 2 speakers (Barnet)].

*Komoro –> Swahili

Kongo is the name applied to a number of closely related **Bantuic** languages spoken in parts of Gabon, Congo, Congo/Zaire and Angola. [This survey: 1 speaker (Brent)].

Konkani is spoken mainly in the Indian state of Goa where it has official status. Alone of the **Indic** languages, it is written with the Roman alphabet. [This survey: 77 speakers (10 Brent)].

Kono is a **Mandic** language spoken in Sierra Leone. [This survey: 7 speakers (5 Lambeth)].

Korean is a language of the **East-Asia** zone spoken in Korea and part of Siberia. It is ranked 17th among the world's languages with some 75m speakers. Korean is written in a conceptually unique script called Hankul which is part syllabic and part alphabetic. [This survey: 496 speakers (167 Kingston)].

Map 20b (on the preceding page) shows that the percentage of Korean speakers in Kingston and Merton is far greater than five times the London average. (About 60% of all Korean speakers live in these two boroughs.) Korean is the top language in Kingston (see Table 5).

Korku is a language of the **South-Asia** geozone spoken in India. [This survey: 1 speaker (Barnet)].

Kpelle is a **Mandic** language spoken in Liberia and Guinea. Although generally written in the Roman alphabet, Kpelle also has its own syllabic script. [This survey: 1 speaker (Islington)].

*Kposo is an **Aframic** language of Ghana and Togo.

Krio, one of the *English-based Creole* languages, is spoken in Sierra Leone (and also in the Gambia, where it is known as *Aku*). [This survey: 321 speakers (87 Lambeth)].

*Krobo is an **Aframic** language spoken in Ghana.

Kru is applied collectively to all the **Kruic** languages spoken in Liberia and the Ivory Coast, as well as to a particular member of this group located in Liberia. [This survey: 5 speakers (3 Merton)].

Kurdish is the name given to a group of related **Iranic** languages spoken in Iraq, Turkey, Syria and Iran. Kurdish is generally written using the Arabic script but with all vowels represented in all circumstances. [This survey: 1,405 speakers (426 Haringey)].

Map 21 (following) shows that an above-average proportion of Kurdish-speaking children are mainly found within a crescent extending from Ealing through central London to Enfield, with others living in Greenwich. While the percentage exceeds five times the London average in Haringey and Westminster, Kurdish is not among the top three languages in any borough.

*Kurmanji is one of the major **Kurdish** languages (see above), spoken mainly in Turkey and Iraq.

Kusaie is a **West-Pacific** language spoken on Kusaie in the Caroline islands. [This survey: 1 speaker (Ealing)].

Kutchi –> Kachchhi

Kwa is the name of four different languages: an **Adamawic** language of Nigeria, a **Bantuic** language of Cameroon, a **Bantuic** language of Nigeria, a **Kruic** language of the Ivory Coast, and an **Aframic** language of Ghana. There is also a **Kruic** language of Liberia called *Kwaa*. In addition, the Aframic and Benuic languages are termed, collectively and respectively, 'Western Kwa' and 'Eastern Kwa' by some linguists. It is thus not possible to identify the precise language of the child reported as speaking Kwa. [This survey: 1 speaker (Haringey)].

*Kwangwa is a **Bantuic** language of Zambia.

*Lahnda –> Panjabi

Lam-nso is a **Benuic** language spoken in Cameroon. [This survey: 3 speakers (2 Haringey)].

Lango is the name of two **Nilotic** languages, one spoken in Uganda (and closely related to Acholi) and the other spoken in Sudan. [This survey: 1 speaker (Haringey)].

Lao is a **Daic** language with official status in Laos. It is written in its own semi-syllabic script which, like the language itself, is closely related to Thai. [This survey: 14 speakers (4 Camden)]

*Lati is a **Daic** language spoken in Vietnam.

Latvian is a **Baltic** language with official status in Latvia. [This survey: 8 speakers (2 Westminster)].

Limba is an **Atlantic** language spoken in Sierra Leone. [This survey: 1 speaker (Greenwich)].

Lingala (Ngala) is a **Bantuic** language spoken in Congo/Zaire and Congo. It is generally known as a second language rather than as a first language. [This survey: 980 speakers (270 Haringey)].

The distribution of speakers of Bantuic languages was given earlier on Map 8. The above-average area for Lingala differs only in that it includes Enfield and excludes Barnet, Southwark and Lewisham. In no borough does it feature among the top three languages.

Lithuanian is a **Baltic** language with official status is Lithuania. [This survey: 178 speakers (34 Ealing)].

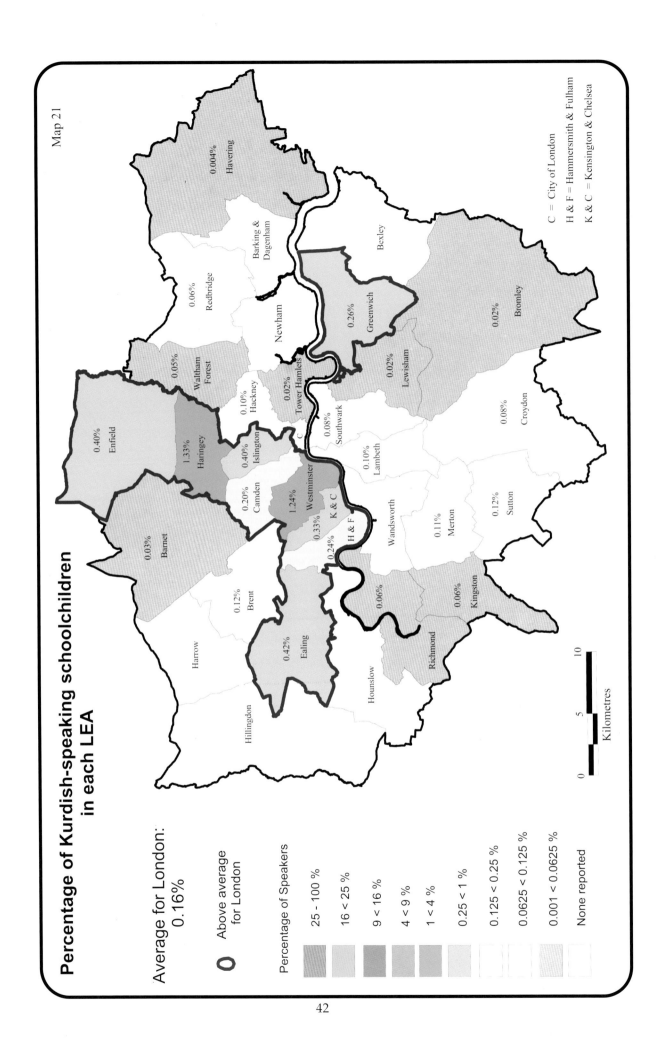

Percentage of Kurdish-speaking schoolchildren in each LEA

Map 21

Average for London: 0.16%

O Above average for London

Percentage of Speakers

25 - 100 %
16 < 25 %
9 < 16 %
4 < 9 %
1 < 4 %
0.25 < 1 %
0.125 < 0.25 %
0.0625 < 0.125 %
0.001 < 0.0625 %
None reported

C = City of London
H & F = Hammersmith & Fulham
K & C = Kensington & Chelsea

0.004% Havering
0.06% Redbridge
Barking & Dagenham
0.05% Waltham Forest
Newham
0.10% Hackney
0.02% Tower Hamlets
Bexley
0.26% Greenwich
0.02% Lewisham
0.40% Enfield
1.33% Haringey
0.40% Islington
C
0.08% Southwark
0.02% Bromley
0.08% Croydon
0.03% Barnet
0.20% Camden
1.24% Westminster
K & C
0.33%
H & F
0.24%
0.10% Lambeth
0.12% Brent
Wandsworth
0.11% Merton
0.12% Sutton
Harrow
0.42% Ealing
0.06% Richmond
0.06% Kingston
Hillingdon
Hounslow

0   5   10
Kilometres

42

Logba is an **Aframic** language spoken in Ghana. [This survey: 2 speakers (Lewisham)].

Logoli (*Maragoli*) is a Kenyan **Bantuic** language.

Losengo is a **Bantuic** language of Congo/Zaire.

Lozi is a **Bantuic** language spoken mainly in Zambia. [This survey: 32 speakers (Southwark;[35] 3 Merton)].

Luba is a **Bantuic** language spoken in Congo/Zaire. [This survey: 2 speakers (Lambeth)].

Luganda (*Ganda*) is a **Bantuic** language of Uganda. [This survey: 816 speakers (176 Haringey)].

The area in which Luganda is spoken by an above average percentage of children is similar to that for the Bantuic languages as a whole (Map 8). The differences are that this excludes Barnet, Camden, Redbridge and Southwark but includes Croydon. In Greenwich and Haringey, the percentage exceeds five times the London average. Lugands is not among the top three languages in any borough.

Lugbara is a **Sudanic** language of Uganda and Congo/Zaire. [This survey: 1 speaker (Hammersmith & Fulham)].

Lui is the name of three different African languages – one **Sudanic** (spoken in Congo/Zaire), one **Nilotic** (spoken in Sudan), and one **Bantuic** (spoken in Zambia). It is not clear which of these is reported in London. [This survey: 1 speaker (Greenwich)].

Lunda is a **Bantuic** language spoken in Zambia. [This survey: 1 speaker (Hammersmith & Fulham)].

Luo and *Lwo* are both alternative spellings for two **Nilotic** languages. They might be distinguished by determining the country of origin or by using their full names Dhopalwo (or Dhopaluo; spoken in Uganda and closely related to Acholi) and Dholuo (or Lwo; spoken in Kenya and Tanzania and closely related to Dhopadhola), respectively. The figure recorded in this survey thus combines both languages. [This survey: 137 speakers (Southwark;[36] 18 in both Haringey and Lambeth)].

Lusoga is a **Bantuic** language spoken in Uganda. [This survey: 8 speakers (5 Greenwich)].

Luvale is a **Bantuic** languages spoken in parts of Angola, Congo/Zaire and Zambia.

Luziba is a **Bantuic** language of Tanzania. [This survey: 1 speaker (Lewisham)].

Lwo –> Luo

Macedonian is a **Slavonic** language, closely related to Bulgarian. [This survey: 32 speakers (15 Ealing)].

Ma'di is a **Sudanic** language spoken in Sudan. [This survey: 4 speakers (Westminster)].

Maghrebi –> **Arabic**

Malagasy is a **Hesperonesic** language with official status in Madagascar. [This survey: 1 speaker (Haringey)].

Malay –> Malay/Indonesian

Malay/Indonesian is a **Hesperonesic** language and is ranked ninth in the world with an estimated total of 160m speakers (of whom this is the first language of

perhaps 50m). Termed Malay in Malaysia and Indonesian in Indonesia, it has official status in both these countries and in Singapore and Brunei. [This survey: 345 speakers (78 Barnet)].

The distribution of the Hesperonesic languages as a whole is shown on Map 17. That of Malay/Indonesian differs from this only in that the above-average areas exclude Haringey, Islington and Merton but add Richmond. The three boroughs in which Malay/Indonesian is best represented are Westminster, Barnet and Kensington & Chelsea.

Malayalam is a **Dravidic** language with official status in the Indian state of Kerala. It is written in its own semi-syllabic script. [This survey: 313 speakers (69 Ealing)].

Malinké is the French name of one of the **Mandic** languages spoken mainly in Senegal and Guinea. See *Manding*. [This survey: 7 speakers (3 Merton)].

Maltese is a **Semitic** language, more specifically a variety of Arabic with considerable influence from Italian and English. It has official status in Malta and, unlike other Semitic languages, is written in the Roman script. [This survey: 118 speakers (19 Lambeth)].

Mambwe is a **Bantuic** language spoken in Zambia and Tanzania.

Mampruli is a **Voltaic** language spoken in Ghana and Togo. [This survey: 1 speaker (Greenwich)].

Mandarin –> Putonghua

Manding is the name of a group of **Mandic** languages spoken in Gambia, Senegal, Guinea-Bissau, Guinea and Mali. These languages include Malinké (see above) and Mandinka (see below).

Mandingo is used in English both as a general name for a group of **Mandic** languages (= *Manding*, see above) and also as an alternative name for *Mandinka* – see below).

Mandinka (*Mandingo*) is a Mandic language spoken in Gambia, Senegal and Guinea-Bissau. [This survey: 32 speakers (Southwark;[37] 5 Greenwich)].

Mangbetu is a **Sudanic** language of Congo/Zaire and Uganda. [This survey: 1 speaker (Brent)].

Maori is a **Trans-Pacific** language with official status in New Zealand. [This survey: 3 speakers (Hammersmith & Fulham, Kensington & Chelsea, Richmond)].

Maragoli –> Logoli

Marathi is an **Indic** language spoken in the Indian state of Maharashtra. [This survey: 49 speakers (19 Barnet)].

Masaba is a Bantuic language spoken in Uganda.

Mashriqi –> Arabic

Mbum is an **Adamawic** language of Cameroon. [This survey: 2 speakers (Brent)].

*Memny –> *Memoni*

*Memon –> *Memoni*

Memoni is reported as *Memny* (1 Lambeth) and *Memon* (4 Ealing). There does not appear to be any language of this name. The word may relate to a group of Muslim traders from Indian known as *meman* or *memon*

---

35   See footnote 16.
36   See footnote 16.
37   See footnote 16.

(with the addition of the Indic adjectival formant -*i*) but this remains to be confirmed.

Mende is a **Mandic** language spoken in Sierra Leone. [This survey: 107 speakers (Southwark;[38] 13 Haringey)].

Mindanao may be an abbreviation of Mindanao-ilanon, a **Hesperonesic** language, or simply a record of the Philippines island of Mindanao as the place of origin. [This survey: 2 speakers (Brent)].

Min-nan (including *Hokkien* and *Teo-Chiu*) is a **Sinitic** language of China and is ranked 24th in the world with some 55m speakers. [This survey: 36 speakers (27 Ealing)].

Moldavian is generally regarded as a dialect of the **Romanic** language, Romanian, but it has the status of official language in the Moldavian Republic. [This survey: 2 speakers (Haringey, Westminster)].

Mongolian is a language of the **Trans-Asia** geozone spoken in Mongolia, Russia (Siberia) and China. It is currently written with the Cyrillic alphabet as well as in its own unique Vertical Mongolian script. [This survey: 45 speakers (24 Kensington & Chelsea)].

Motu is a **Neoguinesic** languages spoken in Papua New Guinea. [This survey: 2 speakers (Brent)].

Mungaka is a **Bantuic** language of Cameroon. [This survey: 3 speakers (Hammersmith & Fulham)].

Nauruan is a **West-Pacific** language spoken in Nauru. [This survey: 1 speaker (Barnet)].

Ndebele is a **Bantuic** language of South Africa and Zimbabwe. [This survey: 13 speakers (5 Haringey)].

Nembe (Brass) is a **Deltic** language spoken in Nigeria. [This survey: 1 speaker (Haringey)].

Nepali is an **Indic** language spoken in Nepal and some adjoining parts of India. It is written in the semi-syllabic Devanagari script. [This survey: 125 speakers (Southwark;[39] 18 Brent)].

Newari is a **Himalayic** language of Nepal which is written in the Devanagari semi-syllabic script. [This survey: 1 speaker (Brent)].

Ngala –> *Lingala*

Ngoni is the name given to an important group of **Bantuic** languages, which includes Xhosa, Swazi, Zulu and Ndebele, spoken in South Africa, Swaziland and Zimbabwe. It is thus not possible to attribute the three speakers of Ngoni reported in this survey to a particular language.

Ngwana –> *Kingwana*

Norwegian is a **Germanic** language, closely related to Danish and other Scandinavian languages, with official status in Norway. [This survey: 92 speakers (Southwark;[40] 12 Ealing)].

Nsenga is a **Bantuic** language spoken in Zambia, Mozambique and Zimbabwe. [This survey: 1 speaker (Haringey)].

Nubian is a collective name for a group of related languages of the **East-Sahel** geozone spoken in Sudan. The single speaker of this reported in this survey cannot therefore be attributed to a particular language.

Nuer is a **Nilotic** language spoken in Sudan.

Nupe is a **Benuic** language of Nigeria.

Nwa is a **Mandic** language of the Ivory Coast.

Nyakyusa is a **Bantuic** language of Tanzania. [This survey: 2 speakers (Haringey)].

Nyang probably refers to the **Bantuic** language of this name spoken in Cameroon. (It is also the name of a **Daic** language spoken in China and Vietnam.) [This survey: 2 speakers (both Lambeth)].

Nyanja –> *Chewa*

Nyankore –> *Runyankore*

Nyoro is a **Bantuic** language of Uganda. [This survey: 2 speakers (Barnet)].

Nzema is an **Aframic** language of Ghana and the Ivory Coast. [This survey: 5 speakers (4 Islington)].

Odual is a **Benuic** language of Nigeria.

Ogori is a **Benuic** language of Nigeria. [This survey: 3 speakers (Haringey)].

Okrika is a **Deltic** language of Nigeria. [This survey: 2 speakers (Ealing and Haringey)].

Olulumo is a **Benuic** language of Nigeria. [This survey: 1 speaker (Haringey)].

Ora is a **Benuic** language of Nigeria. [This survey: 2 speakers (Redbridge and Waltham Forest)].

Oring is a **Benuic** language of Nigeria. [This survey: 1 speaker (Lambeth)].

Oriya is an **Indic** language spoken in the Indian state of Orissa. It is written in its own semi-syllabic script. [This survey: 1 speaker (Barnet)].

Oromo (Galla) is a **Nilotic** language of Ethiopia and Kenya. [This survey: 2 speakers (Barnet and Islington)].

Oron is a **Benuic** language of Nigeria.

Oshiwambo appears to be an alternative name for the **Bantuic** language variously known as *o-she-kwanyama* and *o-vambo* spoken in Namibia (Ovamboland). [This survey: 2 speakers (Barnet)].

Pampangan is a **Hesperonesic** language of the Philippines (Luzon). [This survey: 7 speakers (2 each in Barnet, Camden, and Kensington & Chelsea)].

Pangasinan is a **Hesperonesic** language spoken in the Philippines.

Panjabi (including *Lahnda*) is ranked 13th among the world's languages with some 85m speakers. It is an **Indic** language spoken in the Panjab (on both sides of the Pakistan-India border). Panjabi is written in two different scripts – an adaptation of the Arabic script resembling that of Urdu (used mainly in Pakistan) and the Gurmukhi semi-syllabic script. [This survey: 29,802 speakers (6,971 Ealing)].

Map 22 indicates that there are two above-average Panjabi-speaking areas: a western zone comprising Hounslow, Ealing and Hillingdon, and an eastern zone which includes Waltham Forest, Redbridge, Newham and Lewisham. The greatest concentration is in Ealing with more than five times the average for London as a whole. Table 5 shows that Panjabi occupies first place in nine boroughs – more than any other language – and is second or third in a further five boroughs.

---

[38]   See footnote 16.

[39]   See footnote 16.

[40]   See footnote 16.

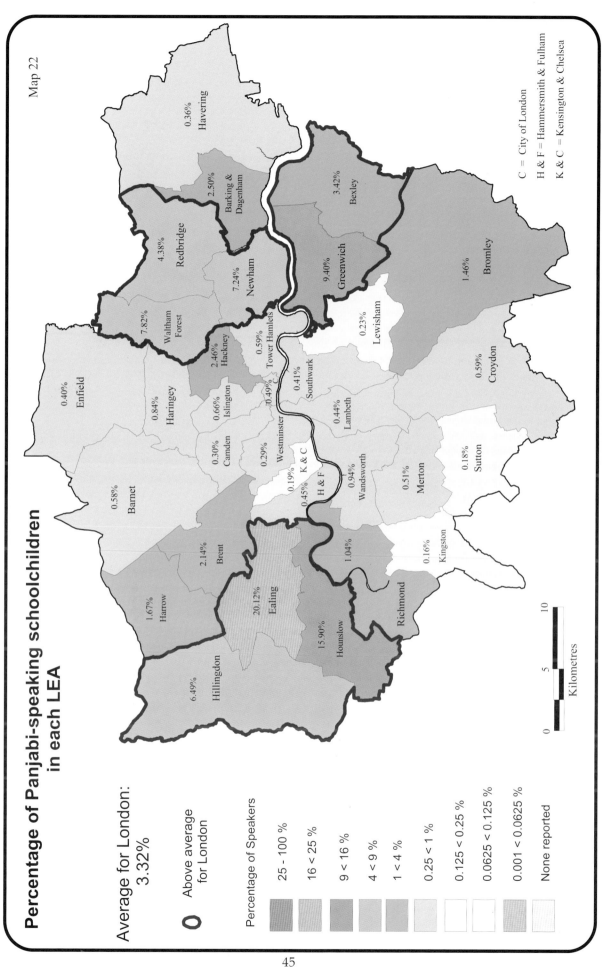

Percentage of Panjabi-speaking schoolchildren in each LEA

Map 22

Average for London: 3.32%

O Above average for London

C = City of London
H & F = Hammersmith & Fulham
K & C = Kensington & Chelsea

Percentage of Speakers

25 - 100 %
16 < 25 %
9 < 16 %
4 < 9 %
1 < 4 %
0.25 < 1 %
0.125 < 0.25 %
0.0625 < 0.125 %
0.001 < 0.0625 %
None reported

0   5   10
Kilometres

Havering 0.36%
Barking & Dagenham 2.50%
Redbridge 4.38%
Newham 7.24%
Waltham Forest 7.82%
Bexley 3.42%
Greenwich 9.40%
Bromley 1.46%
Lewisham 0.23%
Hackney 2.46%
Tower Hamlets 0.59%
Enfield 0.40%
Haringey 0.84%
Islington 0.66%
Southwark 0.41%
Croydon 0.59%
Camden 0.30%
Westminster 0.49%
C
Lambeth 0.44%
Barnet 0.58%
K & C 0.29%
H & F 0.19%
0.45%
Wandsworth 0.94%
Merton 0.51%
Sutton 0.18%
Brent 2.14%
Ealing 20.12%
Kingston 0.16%
Harrow 1.67%
Hounslow 15.90%
Richmond 1.04%
Hillingdon 6.49%

Parji is a **Dravidic** language spoken in India (Madhya Prsadesh and Orissa).

Pashto is an **Iranic** language with official status in Afghanistan which is also spoken in Pakistan. It is written in an adaptation of the Arabic consonantal script. [This survey: 444 speakers (119 Ealing)].

Patwa (Patois, Patua) refers ambiguously to various Creole languages – see *English-based Creoles* and *French-based Creoles* for further information.

Persian –> Farsi

Pidgin probably refers to the Pidgin English spoken in Nigeria and Cameroon (in most cases, as a second language). [This survey: 1 speaker (Barnet)].

Pilipino –> Tagalog

Polish is a **Slavonic** language with official status in Poland. The distribution of the Slavonic languages as a whole in London is shown on Map 24. That of Polish differs only in that the area in which it has an above-average proportion of speakers extends to Hounslow, Richmond, Lambeth and Greenwich. The percentage of speakers is more than five times the London average in Ealing, Hammersmith & Fulham and Kensington & Chelsea. Polish is not among the top three languages in any borough. [This survey: 1,547 speakers (339 Ealing)].

Portuguese is a **Romanic** language ranked 8th in the world. It is estimated to be the first language of some 180m people and to have a total of 200m competent speakers. Although there are marked differences between Portuguese as spoken in Brazil and Portugal, the figures do not distinguish between these varieties. [This survey: 6,051 speakers (1,083 Lambeth)].

The greatest concentration of Portuguese speakers is found in Kensington & Chelsea, closely followed by Lambeth and Westminster (see Map 23). In each of these three boroughs, Portuguese occupies second or third place in Table 5, and the percentage of speakers is more than five times the average for London.

Portuguese-basedCreoles are spoken in Cape Verde islands, Guinea-Bissau, São Tomé & Príncipe, and by small minorities in Hong Kong, India, Malaysia and Singapore. [This survey: 3 speakers (Westminster)].

Putonghua, 'commonly understood language', is the usual name in China for the **Sinitic** language which has official status in that country. This has traditionally been called *Mandarin* in English. It is ranked first in the world in terms of having the largest number of primary speakers (800m) and is jointly first with English with regard to its total number of competent speakers (1000m). Putonghua is written in the Chinese logographic script. [This survey: no precise figure available – see *Chinese* for reasons – but can be estimated as about 900 speakers].

Quechua is a group of languages of the **Andes** geozone spoken in Peru and parts of Bolivia and Argentina. [This survey: 1 speaker (Westminster)].

Rajasthani is an **Indic** language spoken in the Indian state of Rajasthan. It is written in a semi-syllabic script. [This survey: 8 speakers (7 Ealing)].

Rendille is a **Cushitic** language spoken in Kenya.[41] [This survey: 1 speaker (Ealing)].

Romanian, a **Romanic** language, has official status spoken in Romania. [This survey: 40 speakers (9 Ealing)].

Romany is the name of a group of **Indic** languages, varieties of which are spoken in many parts of Europe. [This survey: 75 speakers (45 Hammersmith & Fulham)].

Rundi –> Kirundi

Runyankore is a **Bantuic** language spoken in Uganda. [This survey: 17 speakers (5 Islington)].

Russian is a **Slavonic** language ranked fifth in the world with 170m primary speakers and a total, including second-language speakers, of 320m speakers worldwide. It is written with the Cyrillic alphabet. This survey: 679 speakers (92 Westminster)].

The distribution of the Slavonic languages as a whole in London is shown on Map 24. Russian differs only in that the area in which it has an above-average proportion of speakers also includes Enfield and Bexley. The percentage exceeds five times the average for Russian in Westminster and Kensington & Chelsea. It is not among the top three languages in any borough.

Rutoro is a **Bantuic** language spoken in Uganda. [This survey: 3 speakers (2 Lambeth)].

Rwanda is a **Bantuic** language with official status in Rwanda. [This survey: 47 speakers (15 Barnet)].

Saho is a **Cushitic** language of Ethiopia. [This survey: 33 speakers (Southwark;[42] 4 Tower Hamlets)].

Senga is a **Bantuic** language of Zambia. [This survey: 1 speaker (Hammersmith & Fulham)].

Scottish Gaelic –> Gaelic

Serbian/Croatian (Bosnian). Serbian and Croatian are two near-identical **Slavonic** languages which have official status in Serbia and Croatia, respectively. Serbian is written with the Cyrillic alphabet while Croatian uses the Roman alphabet. [This survey: 659 speakers (137 Ealing)].

The distribution of the Slavonic languages as a whole in London is shown on Map 24. That of Serbian/Croatian differs only in that the area in which it has an above-average proportion of speakers extends to Hounslow and Richmond but excludes Merton, Islington and Haringey. The percentage of Serbian/Croatian-speakers is highest in Kensington & Chelsea where it is well over five time the average, as is also the case in the adjoining boroughs of Hammersmith & Fulham and Westminster. Serbian/Croatian does not feature among the top three languages in any borough.

Sesotho –> Sotho

Shelta is a cant with a substantial **Gaelic** vocabulary. As such, it is rarely anyone's first language. [This survey: 18 speakers (all Ealing)].

Shilluk is a **Nilotic** language of Sudan. [This survey: 1 speaker (Hammersmith & Fulham)].

Shona is a **Bantuic** language of Zimbabwe. [This survey: 257 speakers (40 Haringey)].

Shqipe –> Albanian

Sidamo is a **Cushitic** language of Ethiopia. [This survey: 1 (Ealing)].

Sindhi is an **Indic** language spoken in Sindh (Pakistan) and written in the Arabic script. [This survey: 52 speakers (17 each in Lambeth and Merton)].

---

[41] The spelling supplied by Ealing was *Randise*. This name was not traced but has been assumed to be a typing error for *Randile,* a variant spelling of *Rendille.*

[42] See footnote 16.

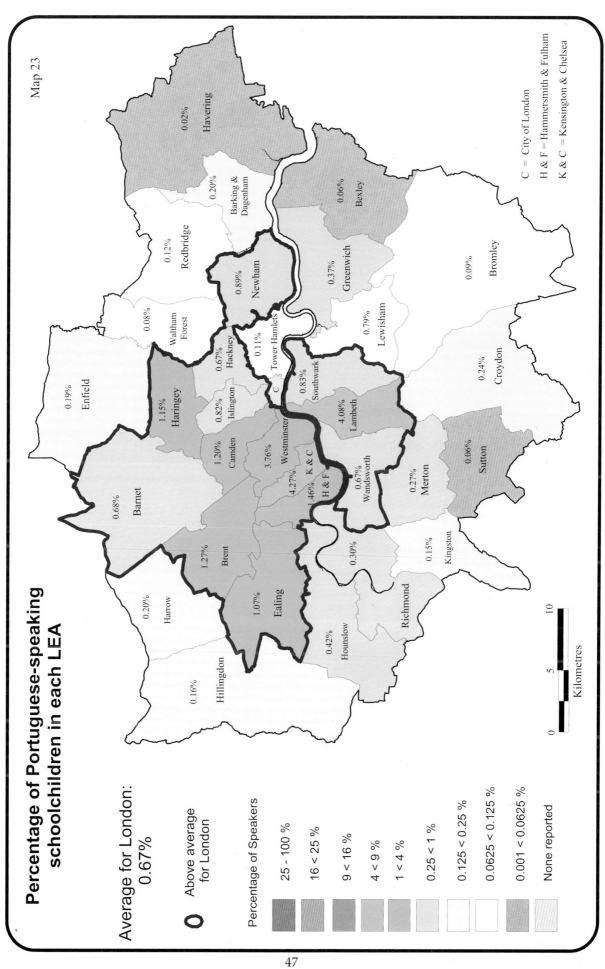

Percentage of Portuguese-speaking schoolchildren in each LEA

Map 23

Average for London: 0.67%

O Above average for London

Percentage of Speakers

	25 - 100 %
	16 < 25 %
	9 < 16 %
	4 < 9 %
	1 < 4 %
	0.25 < 1 %
	0.125 < 0.25 %
	0.0625 < 0.125 %
	0.001 < 0.0625 %
	None reported

C = City of London
H & F = Hammersmith & Fulham
K & C = Kensington & Chelsea

Kilometres
0   5   10

Havering 0.02%
Barking & Dagenham 0.20%
Bexley 0.06%
Redbridge 0.12%
Newham 0.89%
Greenwich 0.37%
Waltham Forest 0.08%
Hackney 0.67%
Tower Hamlets 0.11%
Lewisham 0.79%
Enfield 0.19%
Haringey 1.15%
Islington 0.82%
Southwark 0.83%
Croydon 0.24%
Camden 1.20%
Westminster 3.76%
Lambeth 4.08%
Barnet 0.68%
K & C 4.27%
H & F 1.46%
Wandsworth 0.67%
Sutton 0.06%
Merton 0.27%
Brent 1.27%
Kingston 0.15%
Harrow 0.20%
Ealing 1.07%
Hounslow 0.42%
Richmond 0.30%
Hillingdon 0.16%

47

Singalese –> **Sinhala**

Sinhala *(Singalese, Sinhalese)* is an **Indic** language spoken in Sri Lanka. It is written in its own semi-syllabic script. [This survey: 408 speakers (96 Ealing)].

Sinhalese –> **Sinhala**

The **Slavonic** languages, which include Polish, Russian and Serbian/Croatian among London's top 40 languages (Table 1), all have a similar distribution across London and are mapped collectively on Map 24. The three boroughs with the greatest proportion of speakers of Slavonic languages and in which the percentage is about five times or more the average for London are Kensington & Chelsea, Westminster, and Hammersmith & Fulham.

Slovak is a **Slavonic** language with official status in Slovakia. [This survey: 57 speakers (13 Bexley)].

Slovene *(Slovenian)* is a **Slavonic** language with official status in Slovenia. [This survey: 29 speakers (Southwark;[43] 1 each in Hammersmith & Fulham, Islington, Merton)].

Somali is a **Cushitic** language spoken in Somalia (and also in parts of Kenya, Ethiopia and Djibouti). [This survey: 8,203 speakers (1,375 Ealing)].

Map 25 (following) shows that the area in which Somali is spoken by an above-average percentage of children stretches from Hounslow and Harrow in the west, to Haringey in the north and Greenwich in the southeast. The proportion is marginally higher in Ealing than anywhere else but in no borough does the percentage reach five times the London average. Table 5 shows Somali in second place in two boroughs and in third place in another three.

Sotho *(Sesotho)* is a **Bantuic** language with official status in Lesotho (where the spelling Sesotho is used) which is also spoken in South Africa (where it is written Sotho). [This survey: 10 speakers (5 Barnet)].

Spanish is a **Romanic** language with official status in Spain and many Central and South American countries. It ranks 4th in the world with some 450m speakers (of whom it is the first language of about 400m). [This survey: 5,495 speakers (563 Lambeth)].

The area in which an above-average number of Spanish-speaking schoolchildren live (see Map 26, following) is very similar to that for Portuguese (Map 23), though less extensive. The three boroughs with the highest proportion of speakers are the same for both: Kensington & Chelsea, Westminster, and Lambeth, but only in the first of these is the percentage of speakers as much as five time the London average. Table 5 shows Spanish in third place in Kensington & Chelsea, Lambeth and Camden (but not in Westminster).

A partial explanation for Spanish and Portuguese being best represented in the same boroughs may be that both Kensington and Westminster have many hotels which, formerly at least, employed quite a lot of immigrants from Spain and Portugal, some of whom may have settled in those boroughs. Even so, it is not clear why Lambeth should be especially popular with speakers of these two languages.

Swahili is a **Bantuic** language with about 55m speakers but it is the first language of only about 6m of these (Dalby 1999). It has official status in Kenya, Tanzania and Uganda, and is widely known as a second or additional language in territories adjoining these and in the Comoro islands. Included in the figures which follow are those recorded as "Brava" which is in fact a location in southern Somalia where a variety of Swahili is spoken and from where many political refugees have fled in recent times. (See also *Barawan*.) [This survey: 1,042 speakers (191 Redbridge)].

The distribution of the Bantuic languages collectively across London is shown on Map 8. That of Swahili differs only in adding Hounslow and in excluding Kensington & Chelsea, Southwark and Lewisham. Nowhere is the percentage of Swahili-speakers as great as five time its average for London, nor is it among the top three languages in any borough.

Swati –> **Swazi**

Swazi *(Swati)* is a **Bantuic** language with official status in Swaziland which is also spoken in adjoining areas of South Africa. [This survey: 8 speakers (3 Barnet)].

Swedish is a **Germanic** language with official status in Sweden and Finland (although the first language of only a minority of the population of the latter). [This survey: 181 speakers (37 Richmond)].

***Swiss German** is a distinctive **Germanic** language of Switzerland and adjoining territories.

Sylheti is an **Indic** language, related to Bengali, which is spoken in Bangladesh (Sylhet). See *Bengali+ Sylheti* for details.

Tagalog *(Filipino, Pilipino)* is a **Hesperonesic** language ranked 31st in the world with 40m speakers. [This survey: 1,649 speakers (272 Kensington & Chelsea)].

The distribution of the Hesperonesic languages as a whole is shown on Map 18. That of Tagalog differs from this only in adding Southwark and Merton to the areas with an above-average proportion of speakers, and in excluding Brent. The three boroughs in which the percentage exceeds five time the London average are Kensington & Chelsea (by far the highest), Westminster and Camden, areas which suggest that some of their parents may work in hotels. In Table 5, Tagalog appears only once, in third place in Merton.

---

43   See footnote 16.

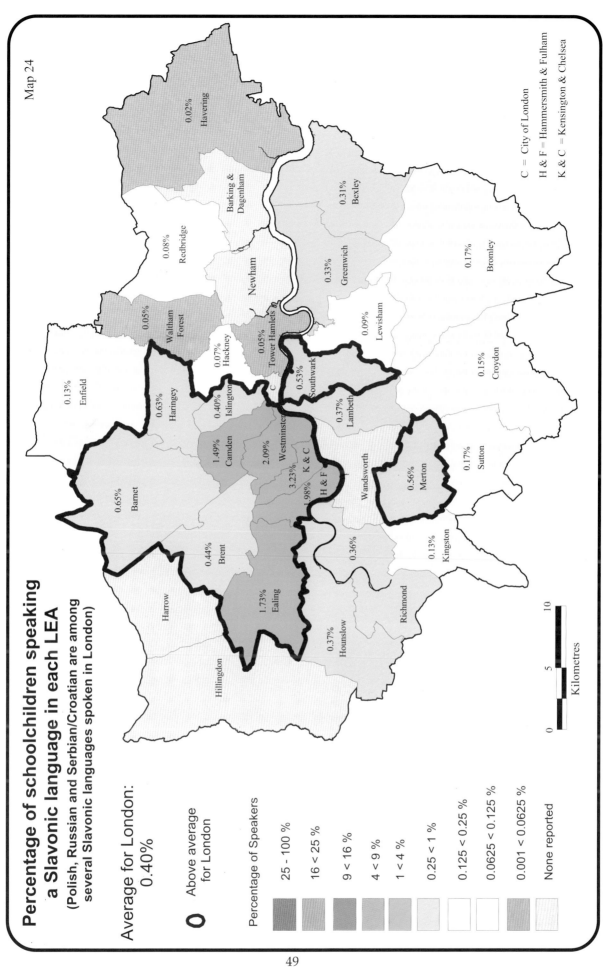

Percentage of schoolchildren speaking a Slavonic language in each LEA

(Polish, Russian and Serbian/Croatian are among several Slavonic languages spoken in London)

Map 24

Average for London:
0.40%

O   Above average
    for London

Percentage of Speakers

25 - 100 %
16 < 25 %
9 < 16 %
4 < 9 %
1 < 4 %
0.25 < 1 %
0.125 < 0.25 %
0.0625 < 0.125 %
0.001 < 0.0625 %
None reported

C = City of London
H & F = Hammersmith & Fulham
K & C = Kensington & Chelsea

Kilometres
0   5   10

Havering 0.02%
Barking & Dagenham
Redbridge 0.08%
Bexley 0.31%
Greenwich 0.33%
Bromley 0.17%
Newham
Waltham Forest 0.05%
Lewisham 0.09%
Hackney 0.07%
Tower Hamlets 0.05%
Southwark 0.53%
Enfield 0.13%
Haringey 0.63%
Islington 0.40%
C
Lambeth 0.37%
Croydon 0.15%
Camden 1.49%
Westminster 2.09%
K & C 3.23%
Sutton 0.17%
Barnet 0.65%
H & F 1.98%
Wandsworth
Merton 0.56%
Brent 0.44%
Kingston 0.13%
Ealing 1.73%
Hounslow 0.37%
Richmond
Harrow
Hillingdon

49

Percentage of Somali-speaking schoolchildren in each LEA

Average for London: 0.93%

○ Above average for London

Percentage of Speakers

- 25 – 100 %
- 16 < 25 %
- 9 < 16 %
- 4 < 9 %
- 1 < 4 %
- 0.25 < 1 %
- 0.125 < 0.25 %
- 0.0625 < 0.125 %
- 0.001 < 0.0625 %
- None reported

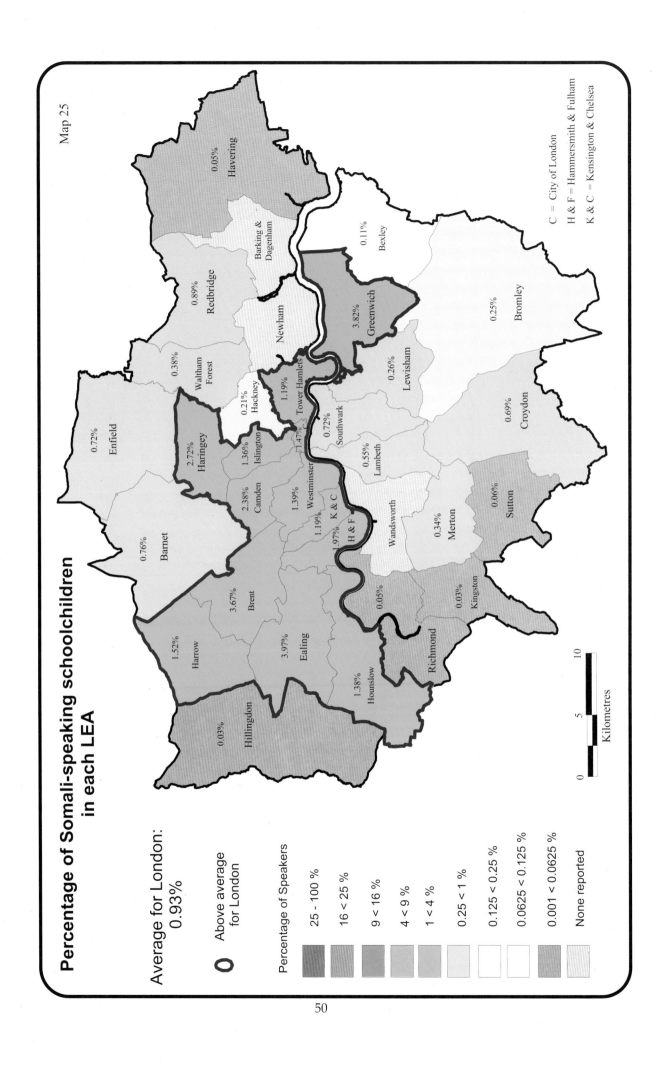

Map 25

C = City of London
H & F = Hammersmith & Fulham
K & C = Kensington & Chelsea

Havering 0.05%
Barking & Dagenham
Redbridge 0.89%
Newham
Bexley 0.11%
Greenwich 3.82%
Waltham Forest 0.38%
Hackney 0.21%
Tower Hamlets 1.19%
Lewisham 0.26%
Bromley 0.25%
Enfield 0.72%
Haringey 2.72%
Islington 1.36%
1.47%
Southwark 0.72%
Croydon 0.69%
Camden 2.38%
Westminster 1.39%
Lambeth 0.55%
Barnet 0.76%
K & C 1.19%
Wandsworth 0.55%
Sutton 0.06%
H & F 1.97%
Merton 0.34%
Brent 3.67%
Harrow 1.52%
Ealing 3.97%
Richmond 0.05%
Kingston 0.03%
Hillingdon 0.03%
Hounslow 1.38%

0   5   10
Kilometres

50

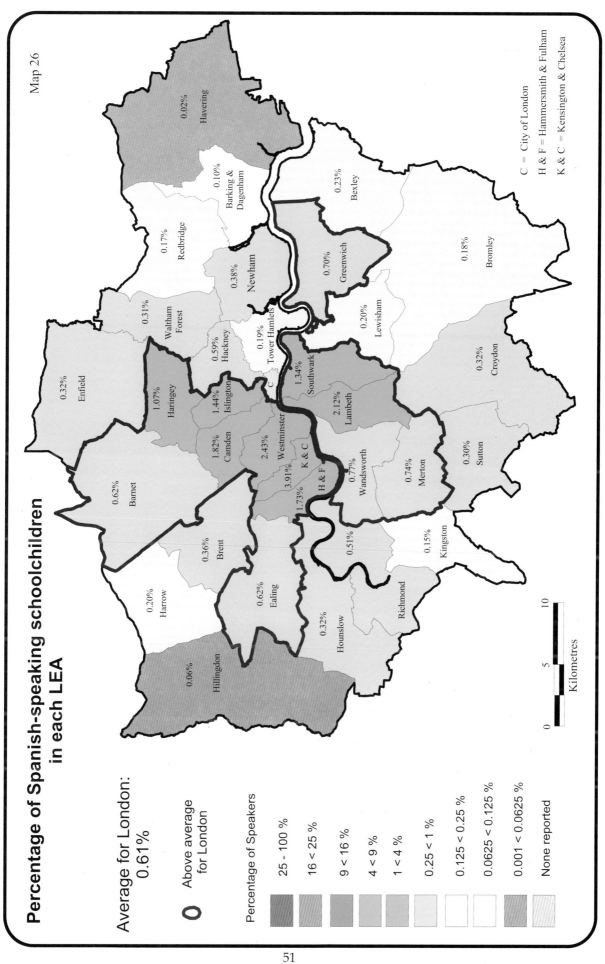

Percentage of Spanish-speaking schoolchildren in each LEA

Map 26

Average for London: 0.61%

○ Above average for London

Percentage of Speakers

- 25 – 100 %
- 16 < 25 %
- 9 < 16 %
- 4 < 9 %
- 1 < 4 %
- 0.25 < 1 %
- 0.125 < 0.25 %
- 0.0625 < 0.125 %
- 0.001 < 0.0625 %
- None reported

C = City of London
H & F = Hammersmith & Fulham
K & C = Kensington & Chelsea

Havering 0.02%
Barking & Dagenham 0.10%
Redbridge 0.17%
Bexley 0.23%
Greenwich 0.70%
Newham 0.38%
Bromley 0.18%
Waltham Forest 0.31%
Tower Hamlets 0.19%
Lewisham 0.20%
Hackney 0.59%
Enfield 0.32%
C
Southwark 1.34%
Croydon 0.32%
Haringey 1.07%
Islington 1.44%
Lambeth 2.12%
Camden 1.82%
Westminster 2.43%
K & C 3.91%
Sutton 0.30%
Barnet 0.62%
H & F 1.73%
Wandsworth 0.77%
Merton 0.74%
Brent 0.36%
Kingston 0.15%
Ealing 0.62%
Harrow 0.20%
Richmond 0.51%
Hounslow 0.32%
Hillingdon 0.06%

Kilometres
0   5   10

51

Tajiki is an **Iranic** language, closely related to Farsi, spoken in Tajikistan, Uzbekistan and Kirghizstan.

Tamil is a **Dravidic** language, written in its own semi-syllabic script, with some 70m speakers, mainly in India (Tamil Nadu), Sri Lanka, Malaysia and Singapore. [This survey: 3,641 speakers (629 Brent)].

Map 27 shows four areas in which there is an above-average proportion of Tamil speakers. Only in Brent does the percentage exceed five times the average for London as a whole. Tamil appears in Table 5 only in Kingston (second) and Merton (third).

Tangale is a **Bauchic** language spoken in Nigeria. [This survey: 7 speakers (all Ealing)].

Telugu is a **Dravidic** language of South India (Andhra Pradesh) with some 70m speakers. It is written in its own semi-syllabic script. [This survey: 13 speakers (3 Ealing).

Temne is a **Melic** language of Sierra Leone. [This survey: 62 speakers (Southwark;[44] 9 Haringey)].

Teo-Chiu -> Min-nan

Teso -> A-Teso

Thai is a **Daic** language with some 45m speakers. It has official status in Thailand and is also spoken in adjacent parts of Laos. It is written in its own semi-syllabic script. [This survey: 346 speakers (34 Southwark)].

Tibetan was the official language of Tibet prior to the Chinese occupation and is spoken by perhaps 2m people there and in neighbouring areas to the south and east. It is a **Tibetic** language and is written in its own semi-syllabic script. [This survey: 6 speakers (3 Islington)].

Tigray -> Tigrinya

Tigre is a **Semitic** language spoken in Ethiopia, Eritrea and Sudan. It is written in the Ethiopic semi-syllabic script, and must not be confused with Tigray (Tigrinya). [This survey: 83 speakers (34 Southwark)].

Tigrinya (Tigray) is a **Semitic** language spoken in Eritrea and Ethiopia which is usually written in the Ethiopic semi-syllabic script. Although Tigrinya is the Amharic name for this language, traditionally called Tigray by its speakers, the Amharic name appears to be more extensively used even in Eritrea where it now has official status. [This survey: 805 speakers (119 Islington)].

Map 28 (following) shows two areas in which an above-average proportion of children speak Tigrinya. The percentage is more than five times the London average in Kensington & Chelsea, Hammersmith & Fulham, and Islington. Tigrinya is not among the top three languages in any London borough (Table 5).

Tiv is a **Bantuic** language of Nigeria and adjoining parts of Cameroon. [This survey: 26 speakers (Southwark only)[45]].

Tok Pisin is an English-based Pidgin/Creole which is the lingua franca of Papua New Guinea. [This survey: 1 speaker (Barnet).]

Tonga is the name of several languages, most of them **Bantuic**, and also an alternative name for Tongan (see next entry). It is thus impossible to know which and how many of these are represented among the reported speakers of this. [This survey: 7 speakers (5 Lambeth)].

Tongan is a **Trans-Pacific** language spoken on the Tonga islands. [This survey: 30 speakers (Southwark;[46] 4 Barnet)].

Tswana is a **Bantuic** language spoken in Botswana and South Africa. [This survey: 3 speakers (2 Lambeth)].

Tumbuka is a **Bantuic** language spoken in Malawi and Zambia. [This survey: 4 speakers (2 Haringey)].

Turi is a **Dravidic** language of India (Madhya Pradesh and Orissa).

Turkish is a language of the **Trans-Asia** geozone which has 60m speakers worldwide, mainly in Turkey and neighbouring countries. [This survey: 15,659 speakers (3,207 Haringey)].

44   See footnote 16.

45   See footnote 16.
46   See footnote 16.

Map 27

Percentage of Tamil-speaking schoolchildren in each LEA

Average for London:
0.41%

O Above average for London

Percentage of Speakers

	25 - 100 %
	16 < 25 %
	9 < 16 %
	4 < 9 %
	1 < 4 %
	0.25 < 1 %
	0.125 < 0.25 %
	0.0625 < 0.125 %
	0.001 < 0.0625 %
	None reported

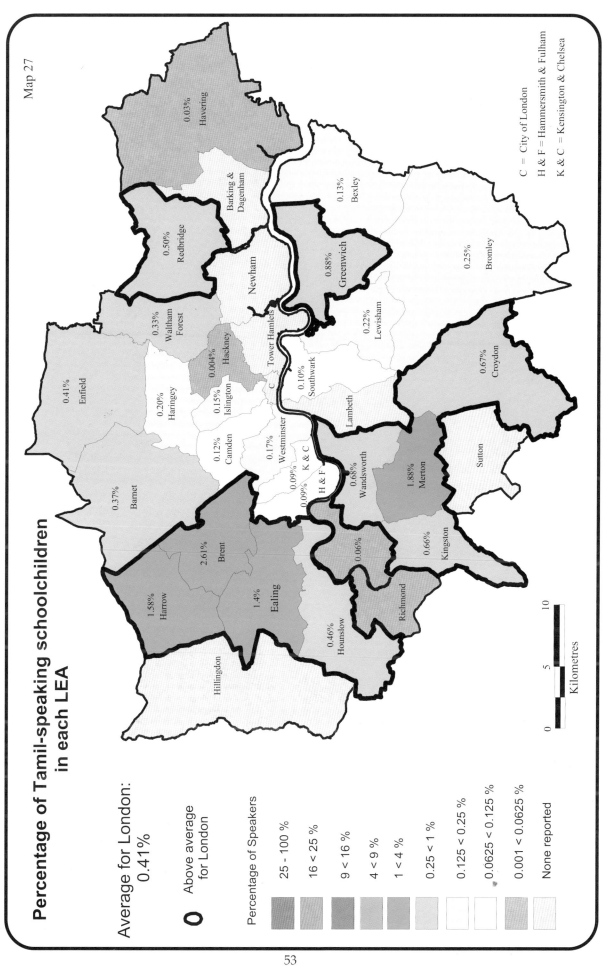

C = City of London
H & F = Hammersmith & Fulham
K & C = Kensington & Chelsea

0.03% Havering

Barking & Dagenham

0.50% Redbridge

Newham

0.13% Bexley

0.88% Greenwich

0.25% Bromley

0.33% Waltham Forest

0.004% Hackney

Tower Hamlets

0.22% Lewisham

0.41% Enfield

0.20% Haringey

0.15% Islington

C

0.10% Southwark

0.67% Croydon

0.12% Camden

0.17% Westminster

Lambeth

0.37% Barnet

0.09% K & C

0.68% Wandsworth

1.88% Merton

Sutton

0.09% H & F

2.61% Brent

0.06%

0.66% Kingston

1.58% Harrow

1.4% Ealing

Richmond

Hillingdon

0.46% Hounslow

0   5   10
Kilometres

Map 28

Percentage of Tigrinya-speaking schoolchildren in each LEA

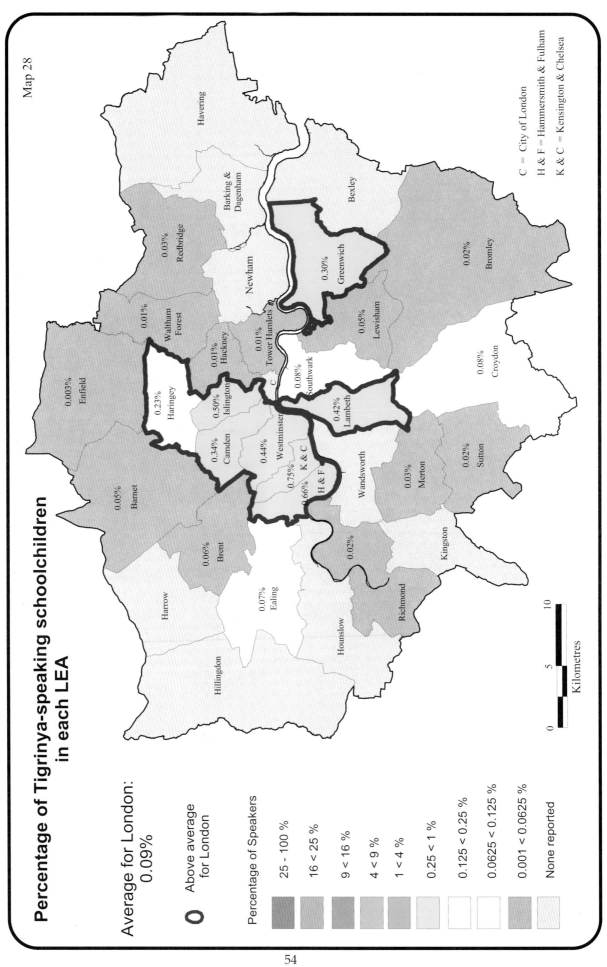

Average for London:
0.09%

O   Above average
    for London

Percentage of Speakers

25 - 100 %
16 < 25 %
9 < 16 %
4 < 9 %
1 < 4 %
0.25 < 1 %
0.125 < 0.25 %
0.0625 < 0.125 %
0.001 < 0.0625 %
None reported

C = City of London
H & F = Hammersmith & Fulham
K & C = Kensington & Chelsea

Kilometres
0   5   10

Havering

Barking &
Dagenham

0.03%
Redbridge

Newham

Bexley

0.30%
Greenwich

0.02%
Bromley

0.05%
Lewisham

0.01%
Waltham
Forest

0.01%
Hackney

0.01%
Tower Hamlets

0.08%
Southwark

0.08%
Croydon

0.003%
Enfield

0.23%
Haringey

0.50%
Islington

0.42%
Lambeth

0.34%
Camden

0.44%
Westminster

0.75%
K & C

0.66%
H & F

0.05%
Barnet

0.06%
Brent

0.03%
Merton

0.02%
Sutton

0.02%
Wandsworth

Kingston

0.02%
Richmond

0.07%
Ealing

Hounslow

Harrow

Hillingdon

The main locations of speakers of Turkish are shown on Map 29 (following). In both Hackney and Haringey the percentage of Turkish speakers is more than five times the London average. Map 30 (also following) shows that, within Haringey, speakers of Turkish are located predominantly in the eastern half of the borough. Table 5 indicates that Turkish occupies first place in three boroughs and is third in a further three.

Turkmen is a Turkic language of the **Trans-Asia** geozone spoken in Uzbekistan, Turkmenistan, Iran, and Afghanistan. It is written in the Cyrillic alphabet in Turkmenistan. [This survey: 1 speaker (Hammersmith & Fulham)].

Twi –> Akan

Ukaan is a **Benuic** language spoken in Nigeria. [This survey: 2 speakers (1 each Hackney and Lewisham)].

Ukrainian is a **Slavonic** language which has official status in the Ukraine. It is written with the Cyrillic alphabet. [This survey: 74 speakers (15 Hammersmith & Fulham)].

Urdu is one variety, written in an adaptation of the Arabic script, of the language known as Hindi when written in the Devanagari script. It is an **Indic** language widely spoken in Pakistan and India. See *Hindi/Urdu* for details.

Urhobo is a **Benuic** language of Nigeria. [This survey: 93 speakers (Southwark;[47] 24 Lambeth)].

Uzbek is a Turkic language of the **Trans-Asia** geozone spoken in Uzbekistan, Tajikistan, Afghanistan and Kirghizstan which has some 18m speakers. It is generally written with the Cyrillic alphabet. [This survey: 10 speakers (5 Hammersmith & Fulham)].

Vietnamese is a language of the **South-Asia** geozone with some 75m speakers, mainly in Vietnam. [This survey: 2,448 speakers (424 Greenwich)].

The above-average area for Vietnamese spreads from Haringey to Lambeth to Greenwich (see Map 31) but by far the highest percentage – far greater than five times the average for London as a whole – live in Greenwich. In spite of this, Vietnamese is not among the top three languages in any borough (see Table 5). Vietnamese is one of very few "top 40" languages for which the borough with the highest proportion of speakers is located south of the Thames.

Visayan –> Bisayan

Wa (Kawa) is a language of the **South-Asia** geozone spoken in Burma and China (Yunnan). [This survey: 1 speaker (Greenwich)].

Wali is the name of three unrelated languages, spoken, respectively, in Ghana, Indonesia and Sudan. The language to which this name refers cannot be established without knowing the country of origin of the child's parents. [This survey: 1 speakers (Haringey)].

Welsh is a **Celtic** language with official status in Wales. As indicated elsewhere in this volume (p 87), the number of children speaking Welsh in London appears to have been seriously under-recorded. [This survey: 66 speakers (14 Richmond)].

Wolof is an **Atlantic** language spoken in Senegal, the Gambia, and Mauritania. [This survey: 130 speakers (Southwark;[48] 17 Hackney)].

Xhosa is a **Bantuic** language of South Africa. [This survey: 11 speakers (2 each in Barnet and Greenwich)].

Yaunde –> Ewondo

Yiddish is a **Germanic** language insofar as it is based on medieval German but it is heavily influenced by Hebrew and is written in the consonantal Hebrew script. [This survey: 16 speakers (11 Barnet)].

Yoruba is a **Benuic** language of Nigeria and Benin with some 26m speakers. [This survey: 10,363 speakers (2,471 Southwark)].

The distribution of the Benuic languages in London is shown on Map 10. Yoruba differs from this only in lacking above-average representation in Lewisham. The percentage of Yoruba speakers is more than five times as great as its London average in Greenwich, Hackney, Lambeth and Southwark. Yoruba is one of the few languages listed in Table 1 which have their greatest density of speakers south of the Thames (in Southwark).

Table 5 indicates that Yoruba occupies first place in two boroughs and second place in three others.

*Zande is an **Ubangic** languages spoken in parts of Congo/Zaire, Sudan, and the Central African Republic.

Zulu is a **Bantuic** language of South Africa. [This survey: 47 speakers (8 Haringey)].

---

47 See footnote 18.

48 See footnote 18.

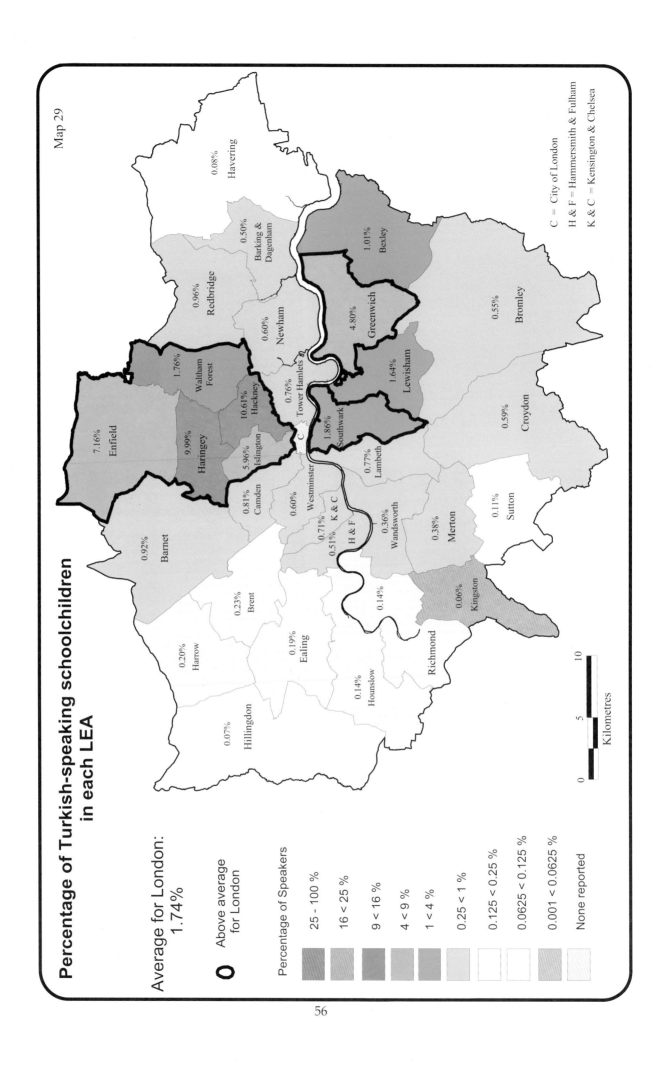

Percentage of Turkish-speaking schoolchildren in each LEA

Map 29

Average for London: 1.74%

O Above average for London

C = City of London
H & F = Hammersmith & Fulham
K & C = Kensington & Chelsea

Percentage of Speakers

- 25 - 100 %
- 16 < 25 %
- 9 < 16 %
- 4 < 9 %
- 1 < 4 %
- 0.25 < 1 %
- 0.125 < 0.25 %
- 0.0625 < 0.125 %
- 0.001 < 0.0625 %
- None reported

0.08% Havering
0.50% Barking & Dagenham
0.96% Redbridge
0.60% Newham
1.01% Bexley
4.80% Greenwich
0.55% Bromley
1.76% Waltham Forest
10.61% Hackney
0.76% Tower Hamlets
1.64% Lewisham
7.16% Enfield
9.99% Haringey
5.96% Islington
1.86% Southwark
0.59% Croydon
0.81% Camden
0.60% Westminster
0.77% Lambeth
0.92% Barnet
0.71% K & C
0.51% H & F
0.36% Wandsworth
0.38% Merton
0.11% Sutton
0.23% Brent
0.06% Kingston
0.14% Richmond
0.20% Harrow
0.19% Ealing
0.14% Hounslow
0.07% Hillingdon

0   5   10
Kilometres

56

Map 30

Haringey: percentage of first language Turkish speakers by postal sector

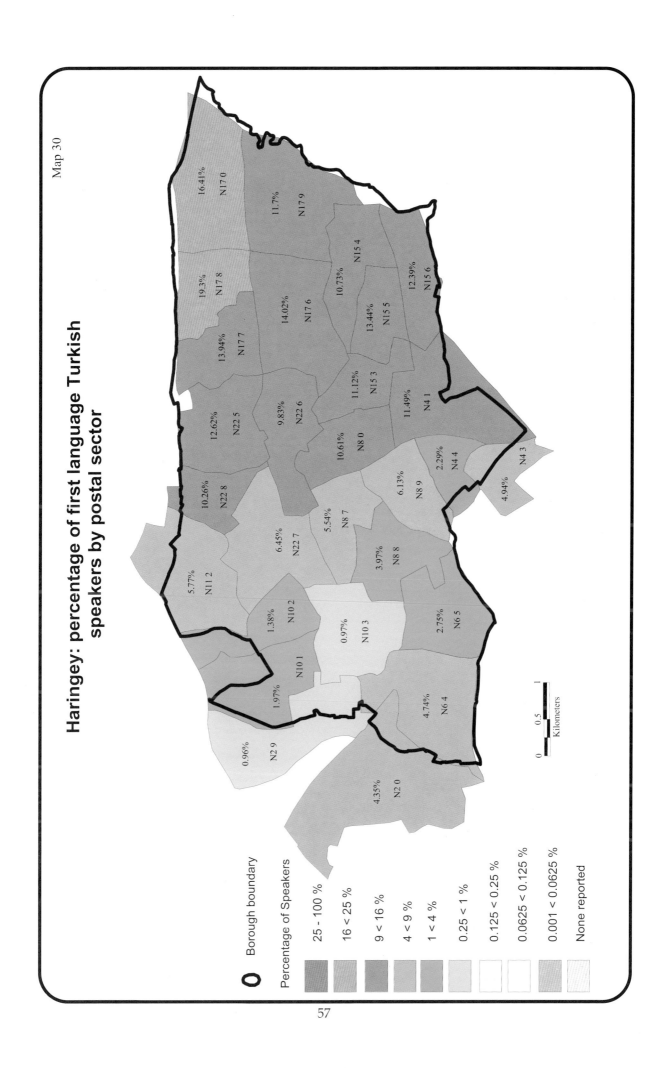

Borough boundary

Percentage of Speakers

25 - 100 %

16 < 25 %

9 < 16 %

4 < 9 %

1 < 4 %

0.25 < 1 %

0.125 < 0.25 %

0.0625 < 0.125 %

0.001 < 0.0625 %

None reported

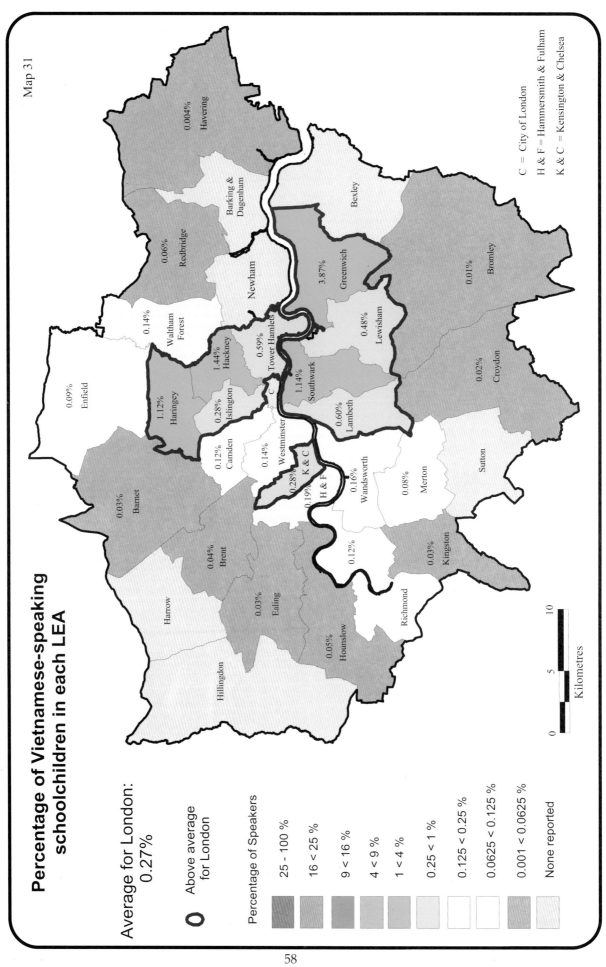

Percentage of Vietnamese-speaking schoolchildren in each LEA

Map 31

Average for London: 0.27%

O Above average for London

Percentage of Speakers

25 - 100 %

16 < 25 %

9 < 16 %

4 < 9 %

1 < 4 %

0.25 < 1 %

0.125 < 0.25 %

0.0625 < 0.125 %

0.001 < 0.0625 %

None reported

C = City of London
H & F = Hammersmith & Fulham
K & C = Kensington & Chelsea

Havering 0.004%

Barking & Dagenham

Bexley

Redbridge 0.06%

Newham

Greenwich 3.87%

Bromley 0.01%

Waltham Forest 0.14%

Tower Hamlets 0.59%

Lewisham 0.48%

Hackney 1.44%

Southwark 1.14%

Croydon 0.02%

Enfield 0.09%

Haringey 1.12%

Islington 0.28%

Lambeth 0.60%

Camden 0.12%

Westminster 0.14%

K & C 0.28%

H & F 0.19%

Wandsworth 0.16%

Merton 0.08%

Sutton

Barnet 0.03%

Richmond 0.12%

Kingston 0.03%

Brent 0.04%

Ealing 0.03%

Harrow

Hounslow 0.05%

Hillingdon

Kilometres

0   5   10

58

References

Baker, Philip 1997 Developing ways of writing vernaculars: problems and solutions ina historical perspective. Tabouret-Keller, Andrée et al. *Vernacular literacy. A re-evaluation.* Oxford: Clarendon Press, 93-141.

—— 1999 Investigating the origin and diffusion of shared features among the Atlantic English Creoles. Baker, Philip & Bruyn, Adrienne (eds) *St Kitts and the Atlantic Creoles.* London: University of Westminster Press, pp 315-64.

Dalby, David 1999 *The Linguasphere Register of the world's languages and speech communities.* Hebron (Wales): The Linguasphere Press. [Including an index of more than 40,000 glossonyms, ethnonyms and toponyms prepared by Michael Mann.]

Daniels, Peter T & Bright, William 1996 *The world's writing systems.* New York: Oxford University Press.

Linguistic Minorities Project 1986 *The other languages of England.* London: Routledge & Kegan Paul

London Education Research Network 1993 *Education in London. Key facts.* London: LBA/ALA.

Miller, Philippa (ed.) 1993 *Floodlight. London's guide to part-time day and evening classes 1993-94.* London: Association of London Authorities & London Boroughs Association.

—— 1999 *Floodlight. the official guide to part-time day and evening classes in Greater London 1999-2000.* London: Association of London Government.

Research and Statistics Unit 1998 London: London Borough of Southwark.

Rosen, Harold & Burgess, Tony 1980 *Languages and dialects of London school children.* London: Ward Lock Educational.

Sinnott, John 1989a *1989 Language Census* London: ILEA Research & Statistics Branch.

—— 1989b *Catalogue of languages spoken by Inner London school pupils.* London: ILEA, Research and Statistics Branch. 5th edition.

Storkey, Marian 2000 Using the schools language data to estimate the total numbers of speakers of London's top 40 languages. *This volume,* pp 63-66.

Philip Baker has worked as Research Director on the Languages of London Project at the School of Oriental and African Studies since its inception in 1993. He is also part-time Research Fellow at the University of Westminster, specializing in the study of Pidgins and Creoles, on which he has published extensively. He has also worked as a film editor and journalist, and in distance education in the UK, Mauritius and Lesotho.

Yasir Mohieldeen gained an BSc in Surveying Engineering at Khartoum University 1992. His GIS expertise was developed during a period working for Hunting Technical Services in the Sudan and the UK. He completed an MA in Environment and Development at SOAS in 1999 where he supports GIS related services,teaching and research in the Department of Geography at SOAS.

Appendix: **List of territories / languages mentioned in this survey**

The list of territories is limited to those known or believed to be the source of (the parents of) some London schoolchildren represented in the survey. These include not only independent countries but also a number of dependent and disputed territories.

The list of languages per territory is also not exhaustive but is limited to those appearing in the alphabetical list of languages (above). Thus the languages listed for Nigeria include 47 currently or recently reported as being spoken by some children in London but not all 400 languages known to be spoken in that country. Numbers in square brackets preceding language names indicate their zones in the Linguasphere classification set out in Table 4.

Afghanistan: [44] Turkmen, Uzbek; [58] Dari, Farsi, Pashto.
Albania: [55] Albanian.
Algeria: [10] Berber; [12] Arabic.
Angola: [99] Chokwe, Herero, Kongo, *Luvale.
Anguilla: [52] English, English-based Creole.
Antigua: [52] English, English-based Creole.
Armenia: [57] Armenian.
Australia: [52] English.
Austria: [52] German.
Azerbaijan: [12] Aramaic; [44] Azeri; [57] Armenian.
Bahamas: [52] English, English-based Creole.
Bangladesh: [46] *Khasi; [59] Bengali+Sylheti.
Barbados: [52] English, English-based Creole.
Belarus: [53] Belarusian.
Belgium: [51] French; [52] Flemish.
Belize: [51] Spanish; [52] English, English-based Creole.
Benin: [19] Hausa; [91] *Bariba, Gurma; [96] Fon.
Bhutan: [70] Jonkha.
Bolivia: [84] Quechua.
Bosnia: [53] Serbian/Croatian.
Botswana: [99] Herero, Tswana.
Brazil: [51] Portuguese; [80] Carib.
Brunei: [31] Malay/Indonesian.
Bulgaria: [53] Bulgarian.
Burkina Faso: [91] *Dagari, Gurenge, Gurma.

Burma: [46] Wa, [75] Jingpho; [77] Burmese; [78] *Karen.
Burundi: [99] Kirundi.
Cambodia: [46] Khmer.
Cameroon: [18] *Bata; [19] Hausa; [52] Pidgin English; [92] Mbum; [98] Ki, Lam-nso; [99] Ewondo, Fang, Mungaka, Nyang, Tiv.
Canada: [51] French; [52] English.
Cape Verde: [51] Portuguese-based Creole.
Caroline Islands: [38] Kusaie.
Central African Republic: [93] *Zande.
Chad: [19] Hausa.
China: [44] Mongolian; [46] Wa; [75] Jingpho; [79] Cantonese, Hakka, Min-nan.
Comoro Islands: [99] Swahili.
Congo: [99] Kongo, Lingala.
Congo/Zaire: [03] Lugbara, Mangbetu; [04] *Alur, Kakwa; [93] *Zande; [99] Bemba, Chokwe, Kingwana, Kongo, Lingala, *Losengo, Luba, *Luvale.
Croatia: [53] Serbian/Croatian.
Cyprus: [44] Turkish; [56] Greek.
Czech Republic: [53] Czech.
Denmark: [52] Danish.
Djibouti: [14] 'Afar, Somali.
Dominica: [51] French-based Creole; [52] English-based Creole.
Egypt: [12] Arabic.
Equatorial Guinea: [99] Fang.

59

Eritrea: [12] Tigrinya, Tigre; [13] Beja; [14] 'Afar.

Estonia: [41] Estonian.

Ethiopia: [04] Oromo; [12] Amharic, Harari, Tigrinya, Tigre; [14] 'Afar, Saho, Sidamo, Somali.

Fiji: [39] Fijian.

Finland: [41] Finnish.

France: [40] Basque; [51] Catalan, French.

Gabon: [99] Fang, Kongo.

Gambia: [00] Mandinka; [52] Aku; [90] Wolof.

Georgia: [42] Georgian.

Germany: [52] German.

Ghana: [19] Hausa; [91] Bimoba, *Dagari, Dagbane, Mampruli; [96] Adangme, Akan (Twi+Fante), Akpafu, Efutu, Ewe, Gã, *Gonja, Gurenge, *Kposo, *Krobo, Logba, Nzema.

Greece: [56] Greek.

Grenada: [51] French-based Creole; [52] English, English-based Creole.

Guinea: [00] Kpelle, Malinké; [94] Kisi.

Guinea-Bissau: [00] Mandinka; [51] Portuguese-based Creole.

Guyana: [52] English-based Creole; [80] Carib.

Hawaii: [39] Hawaiian.

Hungary: [41] Hungarian.

Iceland: [52] Icelandic.

India: [46] *Khasi, Korku; [49] *Kannada, Malayalam, *Parji, Tamil, Telugu, *Turi; [59] Assamese, Bengali, *Bihari, Gujarati, Hindi/Urdu, Kachchhi, Konkani, Marathi, Oriya, Panjabi, Rajasthani; [75] Jingpho.

Indonesia: [24] Itigo; [31] Malay/Indonesian.

Iran: [12] Aramaic; [44] Turkmen; [58] Farsi, Kurdish.

Iraq: [12] Arabic, Aramaic; [58] Kurdish, *Kurmanji.

Ireland: [50] Gaelic

Israel: [12] Arabic, Hebrew.

Italy: [51] Italian.

Ivory Coast: [00] *Nwa; [95] Kru; [96] Abe, Nzema.

Japan: [45] Japanese.

Jordan: [12] Arabic.

Kashmir: [46] *Burushaski; [59] Kashmiri.

Kazakhstan: [44] Kazakh.

Kenya: [04] Dhopadhola, Luo; [14] Rendille, Somali; [99] Bukusu, Gikuyu, Kamba, Kimeni, *Logoli, Swahili.

Kirghizstan: [44] Kirghiz, *Tajiki, Uzbek.

Korea: [45] Korean.

Laos: [47] Lao, Thai.

Latvia: [54] Latvian.

Lebanon: [12] Arabic, Aramaic.

Lesotho: [99] Sotho.

Liberia: [00] Kpelle; [94] Gola; [95] Bassa, Kru.

Libya: [12] Arabic.

Lithuania: [54] Lithuanian.

Macedonia: [53] Macedonian.

Madagascar: [31] Malagasy.

Malawi: [99] Chewa, Tumbuka.

Malaysia: [31] Malay/Indonesian, [49] Tamil; [52] English; [79] Min-nan, Hakka, Cantonese, Putonghua.

Maldives: [59] *Dhivehi.

Mali: [00] Manding

Malta: [12] Maltese

Mauritania: [12] Arabic; [90] Wolof.

Mauritius: [51] French, French-based Creole; [52] English.

Mayotte: [99] Swahili.

Mongolia: [44] Mongolian.

Montserrat: [52] English, English-based Creole.

Morocco: [10] Berber; [12] Arabic.

Mozambique: [99] Chewa, Nsenga.

Namibia: [08] Damara; [99] Herero, Oshiwambo.

Nauru: [38] Nauruan..

Nepal: [59] Nepali; [71] Newari

Netherlands: [52] Dutch.

New Zealand: [39] Maori; [52] English.

Niger: [19] Hausa; [91] Gurma.

Nigeria: [18] *Bata; [19] Hausa, Tangale; [52] Pidgin English; [90] Fula; [91] *Bariba, [97] Ijo, Nembe, Okrika; [98]: Abua, Anaang, Che, Ebira, Edo, Efik+Ibibio, *Eggon, *Ekpeye, Eleme, *Emai, Esan, Gokana, Gora, Idoma, *Idon, Igala, Igbo,
Igede, Ikwere, Isoko, Itsekiri, Kaje, Kalabari, Katab, *Khana, Ki, *Nupe, *Odual, Ogori, Olulumo, Ora, Oring, *Oron, Ukaan, Urhobo, Yoruba; [99] Tiv.

Norway: [52] Norwegian.

Pakistan: [46] *Burushaski; [58] Balochi, Pashto; [59] Hindi/Urdu, Panjabi, Sindhi.

Palestine: [12] Aramaic.

Papua New Guinea: [27] Baining; [34] Motu, [36] Hahon; [52] Tok Pisin.

Peru:[84] Quechua.

Philippines: [31] Bisayan, Cebuano, Hiligaynon, Ilocano, Pampangan, Pangasinan, Tagalog.

Poland: [53] Polish.

Portugal: [51] Portuguese.

Romania: [51] Romanian.

Russian Federation: [42] *Abkhaz; [44] Mongolian; [45] Korean; [51] Moldavian; [53] Russian.

Rwanda: [99] Chiga, Rwanda.

Saint Kitts-Nevis: [52] English, English-based Creole.

Saint Lucia: [51] French-based Creole; [52] English-based Creole.

Saint Vincent: and the Grenadines: [51] French-based Creole; [52] English, English-based Creole.

São Tomé & Príncipe: [51] Portuguese-based Creole.

Saudi Arabia: [12] Arabic.

Senegal: [00] Malinké; [90] Fula, Wolof.

Serbia: [53] Serbian/Croatian.

Sierra Leone: [00] Kono, Mende; [52] Krio; [90] Limba; [94] Gola, Kisi, Temne.

Singapore: [31] Malay/Indonesian; [49] Tamil; [52] English; [79] Min-nan, Hakka, Cantonese, Putonghua.

Slovakia: [53] Slovak.

Slovenia: [53] Slovene.

Somalia: [14] Somali; [99] Swahili.

South Africa: [52] Afrikaans, English; [99] Ndebele, Sotho, Swazi, Tswana, Xhosa, Zulu.

Spain: [40] Basque; [51] Catalan, Spanish.

Sri Lanka: [49] Tamil; [59] Sinhala.

Sudan: [02] *Beri, [03] Ma'di; [04] Acholi, Dinka, Kakwa, Lango, *Nuer, Shilluk; [05] Nubian; [12] Arabic, Tigre; [13] Beja; [19] Hausa; [93] *Zande.

Swaziland: [99] Swazi.

Sweden: [52] Swedish.

Switzerland: [51] French, Italian; [52] German, *Swiss German.

Syria: [12] Arabic, Aramaic; [58] Kurdish.

Taiwan: [79] Min-nan.

Tajikistan: [44] *Tajiki, Uzbek.

Tanzania: [04] Luo; [99] Bende, Gogo, Kahe, Luziba, *Mambwe, Nyakyusa, Swahili.

Thailand: [47] Thai; [78] *Karen.

Tibet: [70] Tibetan.

Togo: [91] *Dagbane, Gurma, Mampruli; [96] Ewe, *Kposo.

Tonga: [39] Tongan.

Turkey: [12] Aramaic; [44] Turkish; [58] Kurdish, *Kurmanji.

Turkmenistan: [44] Turkmen.

Uganda: [03] Lugbara, Mangbetu; [04] Acholi, *Alur, A-Teso, Dhopadhola, Kakwa, Lango, Luo; [99] Chiga, Luganda, Lusoga, Masaba, Nyoro, Runyankore, Rutoro, Swahili.

Ukraine: [53] Ukrainian.

United Kingdom: [50] Gaelic, Shelta, Welsh; [52] English.

United States: [52] English.

Uzbekistan: [44] *Tajiki. Turkmen, Uzbek.

Venezuela: [80] Carib.

Vietnam: [46] Vietnamese; [47] Lati.

West Indies: see under names of the following individual territories: Anguilla, Antigua, Bahamas, Barbados, Dominica, Grenada, Guadeloupe, Jamaica, Martinique, Montserrat, St Kitts-Nevis, St Lucia, St Vincent, Trinidad and Tobago.

Yemen: [12] Arabic.

Zambia: [99] Ambo, Bemba, Chewa, Chokwe, Kwangwa, Lozi, Lunda, *Luvale, *Mambwe, Nsenga, Senga, Tumbuka.

Zimbabwe: [99] Ndebele, Nsenga, Shona.

Section 11: a brief history

John Eversley

The background

Section 11 of the 1966 Local Government Act provided for additional resources to be allocated to local authorities "with substantial numbers of immigrants".[1] The procedure for claiming it required local authorities to use data collected on the languages spoken by schoolchildren. Until its abolition in 1989, the ILEA collected the figures for Inner London; since then each of 32 boroughs and the Corporation of London have collected data. Even the two local authorities which were unable to provide the Languages of London project with data[2] have received Section 11 money.

From 1966 to 1993, Section 11 only applied to immigrants from the New Commonwealth and Pakistan. In 1993 it was extended to all ethnic minorities – in theory. The cumulative effect of changes in the 1980s and 1990s, however, was to increase the number of eligible authorities and populations but, while maintaining, on the whole, existing programmes, in practice London's share of the programme fell, even though the number of eligible people had probably gone up faster in London than in the rest of the country.

Section 11 was originally intended to cover all local authority functions but it became, more and more, an education resource – more than 90% went on education by the time the Ethnic Minority Achievement Grant was introduced in 1999. It was mainly focussed on teaching English as a second language to black and minority ethnic pupils. Looking at the figures for London schoolchildren, it is apparent that, for every three children of New Commonwealth and Pakistani origin, there are two children who speak a language other than English whose families originate elsewhere – see Marian Storkey's article (*this volume*, pp 63-66).

The history

1966: Local Government Act

Section 11 of the 1966 Local Government Act said:

> The Secretary of State [at the Home Office] may pay, to local authorities who in his opinion are required to make special provision in the exercise of any of their functions in consequence of the presence within their areas of substantial numbers of immigrants whose language or customs differ from those of the community...

The legislation applied to England and Wales. In practice only one Welsh authority has received funds.

1967: The formula for defining eligible local authorities

To implement the 1966 Act, the Home Office issued Circular 15/1967 which included, as the Circular

said, "an arbitrary definition of 'differences' and the "additional burden on local authority services". It therefore introduced two methods of "measuring the situation":

> A Commonwealth Immigrant will normally be considered to be a person, adult or child, born in another country of the Commonwealth, who has been ordinarily resident in the United Kingdom for less than ten years and the child of such a person.
>
> To measure the situation in any particular area, the Secretary of State proposes to make use of... [t]he information collected by the Department of Education and Science on form 7.1 [schools] [to derive] the proportion of Commonwealth Immigrant pupils in the total school population... [W]here this proportion is 2% or more, the Secretary of State considers it provides a reasonably accurate guide to those local authorities which fall within the scope of Section 11...

1979: Bill to change eligible populations falls

In March 1979, the Local Government Grants (Ethnic Groups) Bill was given its second reading:

> To authorise the payment to local authorities in Great Britain of grants towards expenditure attributable to the presence of ethnic groups in their area...

Subsection 6 of the bill included a definition of 'ethnic group' which was meant to widen eligibility of the grant beyond immigrants and minorities from the New Commonwealth and Pakistan:

> A group of persons distinguished by colour, race, nationality or ethnic or national origins.

Refugees from Vietnam and Chile were specifically noted as a group which would come within the terms of the bill, as were Poles who had settled in the UK after World War II. On the other hand, as the MP Joan Lestor put it, "I should not expect Lord Pitt... Shirley Bassey, Cleo Laine, Kenny Lynch and Trevor McDonald to receive help under the bill".

In moving the second reading of the bill in parliament, the Home Office minister responsible (Brynmor John) pointed out that 84% of Section 11 spending (by then £33m) was on education. After its second reading and being remitted to Committee, it unfortunately fell at the 1979 election.

1982–86: Changes to eligible public bodies

Following an internal review and a white paper in January 1982, various changes were made to Section 11 in 1982-83. The "ten years" and "2%" rules were abolished. However, eligibility remained restricted to Commonwealth first generation immigrants and their children up to the age of 20, and to Pakistanis born in Pakistan before it left the Commonwealth.

By 1983, spending on Section 11 by central government had reached £70m. The proportion of

---

[1] This article is based mainly on Home Office documents and reports in Hansard. Its terminology reflects Civil Service and parliamentary language of the times to which it refers.

[2] See Baker & Mohieldeen (*this volume*, note 2) for details.

Section 11 in Greater London which was spent on education was 86% by 1984.

Under the 1985 Local Authorities Act, joint authorities were made eligible for the grant and, since then, three Fire and Civil Defence Authorities (not including London) have successfully applied for grants.

In 1986, more changes were introduced, for example, to the way that needs were defined, but spending was still restricted to people of New Commonwealth and Pakistani origin.

By 1986-87, spending had reached more than £83m, of which over 40% was being spent in London.

1988: Inclusion of colleges

The 1988 Education Reform Act made grant maintained schools and further education colleges and polytechnics eligible for Section 11. (The eligibility of polytechnics was taken away in 1993.)

An efficiency scrutiny in 1988 altered various administrative arrangements concerned with Section 11 but it did not change the basic population which was eligible, even though total spending went up from just under £89m in 1988-89 to just under £115m in 1989-90.

1993: Extension to all ethnic minorities

In 1993, the government supported a private member's bill, introduced by Neil Gerrard MP, to extend the scope of Section 11 to all ethnic minorities. The Local Government (Amendment) Act 1993 came into force in September 1993. It also removed the reference to the need for there to be "substantial numbers" of ethnic minority people in a local authority area.

1994-95: Funding transferred to SRB

From April 1994, over half of Section 11 funding was transferred to the Single Regeneration Budget (SRB) in England. (Wales was outside the SRB arrangements.) This was designed to improve the impact of the SRB on ethnic minorities and to put their needs within the broader context of plans for economic development and regeneration. In other words, it was deigned to improve the targeting and allocation of SRB funds to black and minority ethnic communities.

By 1994-95, Section 11 funding was £115m, having peaked in 1993-94 at £131m. Over 90% of spending under Section 11 by this time was on education, with more than 40% of money going to teaching English as a second language in schools to ethnic minority pupils. A further 7.5% of spending was on "non-quantifiable" spending in education such as home–school liaison posts.

The 1994-95 changes also effectively reduced the central government contribution to the costs of Section 11 programmes (essentially salaries and on-costs) from 75% to 50%.

1996-97: The situation prior to the 1997 general election

By 1996-97, spending on Section 11 amounted to just under £88m, of which 70% was funded through the Home Office and 30% through the SRB. Education accounted for over 90% of expenditure.

About one third of spending was through London local authorities with Tower Hamlets the largest recipient (just over £5.2m).

1999: Ethnic Minority Achievement Grant

The Ethnic Minority Achievement Grant (EMAG) was introduced in April 1999 to replace the education element of the Section 11 Grant. It is administered by the Department for Education and Employment. £80m was transferred from Section 11. This has been increased to £130m for 1999-2000 and to £430m over the next three years. This funding is intended to help provide equality of opportunity for all minority ethnic groups. It aims to be more targeted than its predecessor by including additional groups which Section 11 failed to fund. However, EMAG funding is cash-limited and its impact is restricted by (i) the size of the total of available resources, and (ii) the need for authorities to find additional funding to supplement their allocation. Although the grant has been in operation for only a short time, authorities are experiencing considerable difficulties in meeting the match-funded element. This is particularly the case in authorities with high numbers of refugee and asylum-seeking pupils.

Similarly, government provides special grants for services to destitute asylum seekers, and is expected to make funds available for the settlement of refugees following the passage of the Immigration and Asylum Bill. However, the special grants received by London authorities currently only reimburse a proportion of actual expenditure.

Conclusions

In linking Section 11 data to policy planning, the authors of this book are doing something which is a hot topic in central government at the moment. The Centre for Management and Policy Studies in the Cabinet Office is meant to create a resource at the centre of government for "evidence-based decision-making" and for making "joined up thinking and joined up action" a reality. Using administrative data about schoolchildren to plan and implement economic and social policies is an example of what it means in practice. It is particularly significant that the data tell us something about some of the most "excluded communities" in London. The Social Exclusion Unit, also in the Cabinet Office, when working on Deprived Neighbourhoods, became so concerned about the lack of use which is made of existing data that it made better and wider use of routine data one of its priorities. Having seen the potential of such data, the challenge now is to improve the quality and coverage of such data so that they provide a truly reliable source.

John Eversley is Senior Research Fellow in Public Policy at Queen Mary and Westfield College. Prior to joining QMW, he was senior manager in local government and the health service. His research interests include quality and equality in public services and public sector employment and the management of change. He may be contacted at <J.W.R.Eversley@qmw.ac.uk>.

Using the schools language data to estimate the total numbers of speakers of London's top 40 languages

Marian Storkey

1. Introduction

The richness of the language data presented in this volume constitutes a wonderful new resource for studying London's diversity. Other sources allow us to look at very broad ethnic groups, and sometimes data about migrants by their country of birth, but these categories do hide much of the ethnic diversity which exists within these different groups.

One of the questions which is often asked with regard to language data is how many speakers of each language are there in London. This article aims to examine whether it is possible to estimate the total numbers of speakers (of all ages) of each of the top 40 languages using the schools data collected for the Languages of London project.

The issues which need to be addressed are:

- the quality of the data collected;

- an outline of the children in London for whom data were not collected;

- whether the age structures of the different language groups can be constructed in order to estimate adult populations;

- the method of estimating overall numbers; and

- an assessment of the quality of the results.

2. The quality of the data collected

Data have been collected for 896,700 children in London. The quality of the data obtained varies considerably from borough to borough. Two, Bromley and Havering, do not collate figures centrally and were unable to provide language data for their boroughs. Redbridge does not collate language data centrally but was able to provide some information which enabled more reliable estimates to be made. Figures for Waltham Forest were based on a survey undertaken in 1994. Newham's data give numbers of pupils which exceeds the borough's actual number of pupils which implies some double counting or that the database contains records for pupils who have since left.

It is difficult to assess the quality of the data coming from other individual boroughs. Some quality problems were known to have occurred and 3.26% of the records had no language recorded. These included responses which were not given, as well as languages which could not be traced. Problems were known to have occurred because sometimes names of places or countries were given rather than language names, and some typing errors are thought to have been made.

The quality of data of this kind can often improve over time as systems are introduced and initial data collection problems ironed out. For some boroughs the collection of language data was new. If, as is hoped, this study is repeated, we would expect the quality of data to improve over time.

Although there are a number of quality issues with this dataset, it still represents an important resource for London. For many communities, it constitutes the only known source of data which provides information about size and location.

3. An outline of those aged 5-18 for whom language data were not obtained

The official 1998 mid-year estimated population for London of those aged 5-18 was 1,236,600. The difference between the pupils for whom data were obtained and this population estimate is 339,900 The difference between these two figures is made up of a number of components:

- It is believed that language data for 146,500 children in state schools was missed given that there are 1,043,000 pupils in the maintained sector in London (Euteneuer 1999). Some of these are likely to be pupils from pupil referral units and special schools, but the majority have been missed from ordinary local authority and grant maintained schools.

- Pupils in independent/private schools who were not included in the figures supplied by LEAs.

- Pupils in special schools who were not always included in the figures obtained by the Languages of London project.

- Issues about cross-border flows where pupils resident in London attend schools outside of London and vice versa.

- Compulsory education ends at 16 so a number of young people aged between 16 and 18 will be recorded in the resident population but will not be at school.

4. Constructing age structures of the different language groups

If the age structures of the different language groups were known, and if the total number of children aged 5-18 speaking the different languages was known, we could estimate the number of adults and young children who were speakers of each of them, and therefore estimate the total number of speakers of the various languages of London.

The London Research Centre (LRC) produces population projections of different ethnic groups in London which include current age structure break-downs. Ethnic group age structures are produced for the ten ethnic categories recognised by the 1991 government *Census*: White, Black Caribbean, Black African, Black Other, Indian, Pakistani, Bangladeshi, Chinese, Other Asian and Other. The age structure of each language group in London depends very much on the migration patterns of that group. Migrants from abroad tend to be young – mostly in their twenties and thirties. Some young adults migrate with children and older family members, but a large proportion of migrants are young adults. This means that communities such as the Black Caribbean population, which migrated in large numbers in the 1950s and 1960s, now have sizeable populations of older people. Newer communities, such as Bangladeshis, have a smaller proportion of older people. Different ethnic groups have contrasting fertility and migration patterns and this also leads to different age structures. For example, Black Africans tend to have high fertility rates whereas the fertility rates of Chinese people tend to be much lower overall.

Factors were calculated which related the number of 5-18 year-olds to the number of adults and under fives. The factors are shown in Table 1. A factor of 4 indicates that the combined total of adults and under fives is four times as great as the number of those aged 5-18. By assigning the most appropriate ethnic group age structure to each language group, it was possible to obtain an idea of the proportion of the population that school-aged children would represent.

Table 1 Ratios applied to population aged 5-18 to derive adult and under 5 population	
White	5.53
Black Caribbean	4.09
Black African	2.99
Black Other	1.79
Indian	3.51
Pakistani	2.33
Bangladeshi	1.93
Chinese	4.80
Other Asian	4.01
Other	2.36
All categories	4.67
All categories except White	3.05
Refugee population	1.20

Notes

Each factor = Total population less number aged 5-18 / Number aged 5-18

Age structures are derived from 1998 figures (Storkey 1998:1).

The refugee age structure figure is calculated using Home Office data.

5. The calculations undertaken to estimate overall numbers

The first step was to estimate the numbers of children and adults speaking each language from the state school data. An age structure was allocated to each top 40 language group using the age structure of the LRC ethnic group projections thought to best match each language group. The age structure data related the likely ratio of adults and children under 5 to each population aged 5-18. The number of adults and children under 5 was then estimated by applying each ratio to the number of children aged 5-18 speaking each language.

Step two was to estimate the number of language speakers in independent and private schools. There were just under 120,000 pupils in independent and private schools in London in January 1999 (DfEE 1999). No figures are available for the languages spoken in these schools. Ethnic group data of pupils in independent/private schools would give some indication of the representation different language groups outside state sector education but, unfortunately, such data are not collected or not collated centrally by the DfEE. Some potential indirect sources of data exist which help identify the ethnic origin of pupils in the private sector. The first is the *Youth Cohort Study* which records the school participants were attending when they were 15. The second is university admissions data which records ethnic origin and the type of schools applicants have come from. Information on the ethnic data which can be derived from the Youth Cohort Study and the university admissions data will be found in the Annex below. The third possible indirect source – and the one preferred here – is income data. If we assume that propensity of attendance at indepen-dent/private schools is directly related to household income, we can use income data as a proxy measure for attendance of private schools. Because of the biases in the ethnic origin of pupils going on to university education, and small sample sizes in the *Youth Cohort Study*, it was decided to use ethnic group income data as a proxy measure. The variable used was the proportion of households in the top income quintile from the LRC *London Area Transport Study* which recorded ethnic origin and income. The relative propensity of each ethnic group to be in the top income quintile was related to the White group where the White group represented 1.00. Results are shown in Table 2.

Table 2 Relative propensity of each ethnic group to be in the top income quintile (where White = 1.00)	
White	1.00
Indian	0.41
Other	0.63
Chinese	0.74
Black Other	0.37
Black Caribbean	0.26
Black African	0.26
Pakistani	0.26
Bangladeshi	0.07
Source: Anderson & Flatley (1997)	

Weighted percentages were obtained by applying the weights in Table 2 to the percentage of speakers of different languages in state schools. The number of pupils speaking different languages in private and independent schools was then calculated by applying these new weighted percentages to the total number of pupils known to be in private and independent schools. The number of adult speakers of these languages was derived from the pupil figures using the age-structure method outlined above.

The numbers of 5-18 year olds, under fives and adults in the total population had now been estimated. This was still 1,087,000 less than the official mid-year population of London, even allowing for the estimated number of speakers of all the remaining languages spoken in London. This gap could be due to a number of factors:

• Pupils resident in London going to schools outside London (thought to be more likely to be white than ethnic minority children).

• Pupils who have left school at 16 or 17 (more likely to be white than ethnic minority)

- The calculation of adults from the components of the 5-18 population above (more likely to be white than ethnic minority because of the overall numbers in the population)

- Errors in the age structure factors applied to estimate the adult population (direction of bias unknown).

- Pupils missed in the state schools survey (direction of bias unknown).

Two scenarios were examined in order to complete the calculations for numbers speaking each language. The first assumed that none of those in the missing group spoke languages other than English. This gave the highest estimate for English and the lowest estimate for speakers of other languages. The second scenario distributed those whose home language was unknown by the proportions of home languages for pupils in private and independent schools.

Because those missed seemed to be more likely to be white than ethnic minority, a weighting was applied to the study language percentages where English was given a weight of 100% and all other languages a weight of 25%. The percentages were recalculated and then applied to the number of unknown speakers (1,087,000). All these components were then added together. The numbers are shown in Table 3.

There are a number of differences between the ranking of languages in Table 3, which relate to speakers of all ages, and the ranking of the same languages given by Baker & Mohieldeen (*this volume*, p 3, Table 1), which relate to schoolchildren only. Such differences are due to the contrasting age structures of the various language groups. For example, the Bangla-deshi community has a younger age structure than that of speakers of the languages which comprise the Indian ethnic group. In consequence, the Indian ethnic group has a higher ratio of adults to school-children than does the Bangladeshi group. This is why Bengali+Sylheti is ranked second in Baker & Mohieldeen's table (where only schoolchildren were considered) but moves down to fifth place in Table 3 here (where speakers of all ages are taken into account).

6. An assessment of the quality of the data

From the text, it can be seen that very broad assumptions have been made in order to estimate the total number of speakers of different languages. In fact, the data collected only represent 13% of all of London's residents so the vast majority of Londoners have had their home language estimated. There are many unknowns in these calculations: in particular, the languages spoken by pupils in independent/private schools are unknown, as are the age structures of different language groups, i.e. whether some languages are more or less likely to be spoken by children or adults. However, the overall figures do give a fairly good indication of the number of speakers of each language.[1] and improved data

collection in the future will enable more reliable estimates to be made.

rank	language	scenario A	scenario B
	Table 3		
	Estimated total numbers of speakers		
	(to the nearest hundred)		
	of the top 40 languages in London		
1	English	5,737,400	5,636,500
2	Panjabi	143,600	155,700
3	Gujarati	138,000	149,600
4	Hindi/Urdu	125,900	136,500
5	Bengali+Sylheti	119,900	136,300
6	Turkish	67,600	73,900
7	Arabic	49,500	53,900
8	English Creoles	46,300	50,700
9	Cantonese	45,100	47,900
10	Yoruba	43,300	47,600
11	Greek	28,600	31,100
12	Portuguese	26,900	29,400
13	French	25,300	27,600
14	Akan (Twi+Fante)	25,000	27,500
15	Spanish	24,500	26,700
16	Somali	19,037	22,343
17	Tamil	17,700	19,200
18	Vietnamese	15,800	16,800
19	Farsi	14,900	16,200
20	Italian	11,300	12,300
21	Tagalog	8,600	9,300
22	Igbo	8,200	9,000
23	French Creoles	7,700	8,400
24	Polish	6,600	7,200
25	Kurdish	6,200	6,800
26	Swahili	4,500	4,900
27	Lingala	4,100	4,500
28	Japanese	4,000	4,300
29	Albania	3,900	4,200
30	German	3,600	3,900
31	Luganda	3,400	3,700
32	Gã	3,400	3,700
33	Russian	3,200	3,500
34	Serbian/Croatian	3,100	3,400
35	Korean	3,000	3,200
36	Hebrew	2,800	3,100
37	Sinhala	2,200	2,300
38	Tigrinya	1,900	2,300
39	Pashto	1,600	1,700
40	Amharic	1,000	1,200

Note: These figures should be treated with caution. They are estimates which have been calculated by making a large number of assumptions. Please see accompanying text for methodology.

Scenario A assumes all those outstanding unknowns after calculations have English as their first language.

Scenario B assumes that 91% of all those outstanding unknowns after calculations have English as their first language and that the others have first languages in proportion to the schools study percentages (see text for fuller explanation).

Marian Storkey is Principal Research Officer at the London Research Centre.

For information about LRC, visit its website at <www.london-research.gov.uk>.

---

[1] With the exception of both the English and French Creoles for which the data collected are especially susceptible to error. See the entries for these in the alphabetical list of languages in Baker & Mohieldeen (*this volume*) for details.

References

Anderson, Harriet & Flatley, John 1997 *Contrasting London incomes*. London: London Research Centre.

Baker, Philip & Mohieldeen, Yasir 2000 The languages of London's schoolchildren. *This volume*, pp 5-60.

Department for Education and Employment 1998 *The Youth Cohort Study: the activities and experiences of 16 and 18 year olds in England and Wales*. London: The Stationery Office.

—— 1999a *Statistics of education. Schools in England 1999*. London: The Stationery Office.

—— 1999b Press release 152/99. 1 April 1999.

DfEE = Department for Education and Employment.

Euteneuer, Ric 1999 *Key facts for London 1999*. London: London Research Centre.

London Research Centre 1991 London area transport study. Unpublished report commissioned by the Department of Transport and the London boroughs. [The data from this study which are cited in this article can be found in Anderson & Flatley 1997.]

Storkey, Marian 1998 *Round ethnic group projections*. London: London Research Centre.

Annex: **Estimates of percentages of ethnic groups attending state and independent schools**

The Youth Cohort Study (YCS; DfEE 1998) is a programme of surveys conducted by the Department for Education and Employment that contact a sample of an academic year group or "cohort" of young people in the spring following completion of compulsory education, and again two years later. The first YCS survey was conducted in 1985.

Figures below were obtained from a specially commissioned tabulation from the Youth Cohort Study 9, Sweep 1.

Ethnic group by school type			
Ethnic group	Total percentage*	School type state	independent
Total	100%	100%	100%
White	88%	88%	88%
Black	2%	2%	**
(Total Asian	7%	7%	9%)
Indian	3%	3%	4%
Pakistani	2%	2%	1%
Bangladeshi	1%	1%	**
Other Asian incl. Chinese	1%	1%	3%
Other ethnic group	2%	2%	1%
Not answered	1%	1%	1%

* All percentages rounded to nearest whole number.
** Less than 0.5%.

Note: The above figures should be treated with caution as some are based on small numbers.

The figures in the table above show that, of the young people in the study, the same proportion of Whites were from state schools as from independent schools (although, of course, there would be far greater numbers in the state sector). Other Asians (including Chinese) and Indians had higher proportions from the independent sector, whereas there were smaller proportions of Black, Pakistani and Bangladeshis from the independent sector.

These figures are national figures. The numbers in the study would not provide robust data at regional level, and it was thus not possible to obtain data for London from this source.

Youth Cohort Study figures for England and Wales issued by the DfEE (1999b) additionally showed that:

> Asian youngsters, particularly Indians, were more likely to be studying for higher education qualifications that White youngsters, and more likely to be studying for a qualification overall.

> Among 16 year-olds, 67% of Whites are in full-time education compared with 82% of Blacks and 86% of Asians.

> Relatively few Black youngsters were studying for a higher education qualification (11%) although they were more likely than White young people to be studying for vocational qualifications.

A further commissioned tabulation was obtained from the Universities and Colleges Admissions Service (UCAS), reproduced below.

Accepted applicants within Greater London, by ethnic origin and previous educational establishment		
Ethnic origin	Independent sector	State sector
Bangladeshi	1.1%	2.8%
Chinese	3.2%	2.0%
Indian	10.9%	13.4%
Pakistani	1.9%	4.3%
Other Asian	4.4%	4.4%
Black African	2.1%	8.2%
Black Caribbean	0.7%	4.8%
Other	0.4%	2.2%
White	66.1%	44.5%
Other	4.5%	5.4%
Not known	4.8%	8.0%
Total	100.0%	100.0%

(UCAS special tabulation run November 1999)

The above table shows that all ethnic minority groups, apart from Chinese and other Asian, had higher proportions for those going to university from state schools than from independent schools. If people from each ethnic group had the same propensity to go to university, regardless of whether they were educated in the state or independent sector, these figures would suggest that much lower proportions of Bangladeshis, Pakistanis, Black Africans, Black Caribbeans and people from other ethnic groups were in the independent sector. If we could justify this assumption, we could create factors from these figures which would relate ethnic group in state and independent sectors, and which could then be applied to ethnic origin of all those in state schools in order to estimate ethnic origin of all those in independent schools.

The educational performance of London pupils in context

Ian McCallum

The ability to collect and interpret social information has been greatly enhanced by developments in information technology (IT). The value of such information to the community at large depends on how well it can be summarised and presented.

Geographical areas, housing and GCSE results

The accompanying map shows one way in which IT can be used to display one aspect of the complex relationships between GCSE results and some contextual information. The percentage of house-hold heads in Local Authority (LA) or Housing Association (HA) property is one of the influences which, together with the quality of teaching, levels of LEA support, parental education and many other contextual variables, may be associated with good GCSE results. In this example, the percentages of household heads in LA or HA homes have been presented in four broad categories, each with eight boroughs. Boroughs with the lowest percentages are shown in red and those with the highest are shown in blue. Red circles have been used to identify the eight boroughs with the best GCSE results and blue circles to identify the eight with the worst results. Circle diameters are proportional to the percentages of pupils achieving five or more A* to C grades.

The map provides a clear indication that boroughs with the lowest percentages of LA or HA tenants tend also to be those with the best GCSE results and *vice versa*. It does not, of course, provide any indication of the reasons for the association. Housing is only one of many factors that could be related to GCSE performance and, although this relationship is strong, it is, of course, not a perfect one. This is borne out by the performances of Sutton, Lewisham, Camden and Greenwich which do not conform to the general pattern. The map is, however, very valuable in challenging the assumption that local authorities in London are solely responsible for the relative performance of their schoolchildren.

Ethnicity, housing and GCSE results

Some London boroughs maintain comprehensive and accessible pupil records and are therefore able to make these available for research. A few of these now also record pupil home postcodes which can be used, in conjunction with information from the 1991 census, to describe some of the characteristics of the immediate area (the enumeration district or ED) of each pupil's home.

A confidential report to one London borough drew on pupil records that included information on ethnicity, Key Stage 3 and GCSE performance of its 1998 cohort of pupils. This indicated that, although ethnic minority pupils performed less well than white pupils at Key Stage 3, their performance at GCSE level was superior. Table 1 shows the extent of these educational performance differences, all of which are significant (P<.05).

| | | Key Stage 3 performance | | | GSCE performance | |
| | | | | | Average no. | Average |
Pupils	N*	English	Maths	Science	of A* - Cs	GCSE score
White	506	4.85	4.71	4.63	4.23	37.48
Ethnic minority	994	4.37	4.37	4.29	4.69	39.76
Unknown	394	4.58	4.19	4.39	4.62	40.21
All	1894	4.54	4.42	4.40	4.54	39.16

Table 1
Pupil Key Stage 3 average levels and GCSE performance by ethnic group

Differences in the levels of performance, although statistically significant, are small and could be considered to be the result of other factors associated with ethnicity.

The average characteristics of the ED in which homes of pupils recorded as white and those recorded as belonging to an ethnic minority were calculated and were found to be significantly different (P>=0.005). Ethnic minority pupils lived in areas in which an average of 68% of homes were owner occupied compared with 65% of white pupils. All the other differences indicated that, in general, the ethic minority pupils came from locations with less favourable characteristics. The extent of these differences is shown in Table 2.

The better performance of the ethnic minority pupils appears to be in spite of their homes being located in areas with characteristics that could reasonably be considered to be "less advantageous" than those of their white counterparts. These findings may, of course, be unique, to this one London borough; they have, however, been used to show the type of exploratory study that can be undertaken with fairly modest IT resources and appropriate pupils records. They are, nevertheless, of value because they illustrate the complexity of the issues associated with educational performance as well as the dangers inherent in some current misleading assumptions.

Percentages in Local Authority or Housing Association housing - 1998 percentages with 5 GCSEs

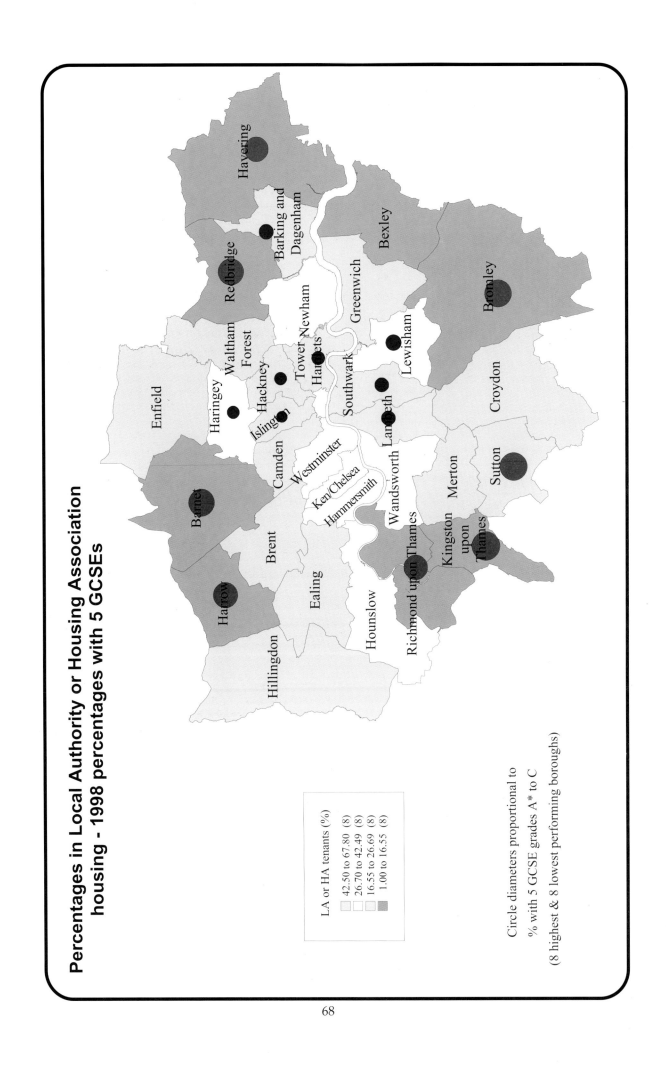

LA or HA tenants (%)

42.50 to 67.80 (8)
26.70 to 42.49 (8)
16.55 to 26.69 (8)
1.00 to 16.55 (8)

Circle diameters proportional to
% with 5 GCSE grades A* to C
(8 highest & 8 lowest performing boroughs)

Table 2						
Social background of home ED by pupils' ethnic group						
		Household heads with children in social class:				
Pupils	Number	I & II	IV & V	Qualified	Unemployed	Overcrowded
White	629	37.95%	15.94%	13.72%	10.71%	4.54%
Ethnic minority	1014	30.19%	22.22%	12.16%	13.13%	8.28%
Unknown	186	21.04%	28.85%	7.58%	16.89%	14.88%
All	1829	31.93%	20.73%	12.23%	12.68%	7.66%

(The 3% decrease in the numbers compared with Table 1 arises because some postcodes were incomplete.)

School level performance

It is probable that, in general, well-qualified parents with good resources have an advantage in terms of the levels of educational support that they can provide for their children. If some schools include disproportionately small numbers of pupils from such homes, they may be subject to criticism when their performance is seen to be poorer than that of other schools.

In order to examine this aspect of pupil backgrounds, schools were ranked in order of the average percentages of adults qualified to diploma level (percent qualified) in pupil home EDs. The average number of GCSE grade A* to C passes and background characteristics of pupils at the two schools with the highest and lowest ranks are shown in Table 3.

Table 3						
GCSE performance of schools with pupils from different backgrounds						
	average no.	Household head with children in social class:				
%qualified	of A*-C	I & II	IV & V	Qualified	Unemployed	Overcrowded
Greatest	6.96%	49.92%	13.65%	23.17%	9.86%	3.71%
Least	2.88%	26.435	21.69%	7.10%	11.70%	5.14%
(N>=112)						

There is a dramatic difference – 23% versus 7% – in the percentages of qualified adults in the home EDs of pupils in these two schools. Differences in average backgrounds are as expected, with the "most favourable" measures associated with schools with the greatest percentages qualified to diploma level or higher. Pupils at the lowest ranked school averaged more than twice as many GCSE passes as those at the lowest ranked school.

These data illustrate extreme differences between the backgrounds and educational performance of pupils in two schools. Similar orders of difference were also apparent in the GCSE results of each of the schools in the highest and lowest three ranks.

Summary

Information from one local authority has been used to illustrate some of the potential value to be derived from the use of available mapping and other software. The use of such procedures enables findings drawn from complex data to be presented in a way that conveys insights quickly and effectively to a wide audience.

In spite of the comprehensive nature and ready availability of the data on which these findings are based, they are not as complete as is desirable and their restriction to only one area means that they should be treated with some caution. Nevertheless, they provide justification for the maintenance of comprehensive records that can be explored, interpreted and presented using currently available IT.

The recording of data on languages spoken by pupils with English as a second language, together with other relevant data, in standard format would facilitate the identification of disadvantage, or success, associated with any range of factors. If widely introduced, greater confidence could be placed in findings derived from the resulting increased database. Information from the next census, due in 2001, will soon supersede that from the 1991 census. This, with an appropriate database and suitable software, would enable those with even quite modest personal computers to undertake demographic research previously achievable only by research organisations with substantial resources.

Ian McCallum was Director of the Research and Development Unit at Garnett College of Education. His research into the backgrounds, aptitudes and abilities at 19 further education colleges led to a DPhil in 1980. He has since worked as Senior Research Officer at the Council for National Academic Awards and as Principal Research Officer at the London Research Centre. He now works as an educational consultant. For further information, he may be contacted at <IMcCallum@compuserve.com>.

Languages speak volumes for global business

Andy Land

As the global economy becomes ever more integrated, and advances in information and communications technology allow business to be carried out in different and disparate places, location is becoming a crucial issue for companies and organisations. After the USA, Britain is the world's most successful country at attracting international investment. London, in turn, attracts more international companies than any other European city.

There are many reasons for London's success. An annual survey of senior European business executives points to some of these – the ease of access to markets, customers and clients; the availability of office space; the quality of tele-communications; the ease of travelling around the city, the excellent transport links with other areas; and the availability of language skills (*Healey & Baker European Cities Monitor 1999*).

The availability of language skills is becoming a key driver for many companies. More than a fifth of senior European business executives identified this an "absolutely essential" factor in deciding where to locate their business (*Healey & Baker European Cities Monitor 1999*). This is particularly true of many of the "value-added" projects that London seeks to attract. Pan-European customer service centres, for example, which provide telephone-based services directly to customers in a number of countries, often require telephone agents who are native speakers of the required languages. European Headquarters, which exercise co-ordination and control functions over geographically-dispersed operations, need staff with well developed language skills across a whole range of functions, including marketing, sales, human resources, finance and IT.

London is unique in Europe in being able to provide such a large, skilled, multilingual labour force. This is almost entirely due to the cosmo-politan nature of the population. Research in this publication shows that almost one third of London's schoolchildren have a language other than English as their first. 24% of Londoners were born outside of the UK, of whom 378,000 were born in other European Union countries (*Labour Force Survey*, February 1999).

Many major international companies have chosen London because of the availability of such staff. Delta Air Lines, for example, decided to consolidate their 14 European-wide call centres into one, based in West London. Mike Boynton, regional director for Reservations Sales Europe, stated that London was selected "because we felt the economic climate and the large multilingual workforce were important keys to our success. We had no diffi-culties in recruiting staff equipped with language skills of mother-tongue standard for each of the 14 European countries that Delta's London call centre now represents". Similarly, Air France chose to locate its European call centre in London ahead of two other European cities because, as Frédéric Verdier, European Call Centre Director, says: "London is one of the world's most cosmopolitan

cities and is ideal for the recruitment of multilingual staff". Japan Airlines have recently expanded their London-based operation. Of the 45 people they have recruited, 20 are Japanese speakers while the remaining 25 have at least two European languages.

The languages most in demand are, not surprisingly, those from western Europe and, in particular, French and German, Spanish and Portuguese, Italian and the Scandinavian languages. There is also an increasing demand for East European languages. However, international investors are coming to London from many other parts of the world – in particular South-East Asia and the Indian subcontinent – so there is often a demand for a diverse range of languages.

London's claim to have one of the most multilingual populations in the world plays a key role in persuading companies to consider this city as a business location but it is very important to be able to back this up with hard evidence. We already have data from the 1991 census that tell us the numbers of people born in a particular country. We also know the number of students studying languages at degree level in London. The Languages of London project has built on this knowledge, providing in this publication – for the first time – indications of the numbers of native speakers of some 300 languages who live in London, whether born here or abroad.

When, in September 1999, Tony Blair launched the London First Global Network, an initiative promoting London as the world's most multi-cultural city for doing business, he rightly stressed that "London's diversity helps it to compete in today's global market place". The Languages of London report greatly enhances London's ability to promote itself, powerfully, as Europe's best business location for international companies.

References

Healey & Baker European Cities Monitor 1999. London: Healey & Baker.

Labour Force Survey. London: Department of Trade and Industry, February 1999.

Andy Land is Information Manager at London First Centre, the inward investment agency for London. London First Centre provides a free and con-fidential consultancy service to companies and associations considering London as a business location. For further details, phone 020 7925 2000 or visit the Centre's website at <www.lfc.co.uk>

Languages and the Square Mile

Tim Connell

THE ORGAN GRINDERS' QUARTERS NEAR HATTON GARDEN

1. Introduction

The City of London is a major financial trading centre for reasons of both history and geography. It was the driving force behind mercantile expansion betweem the 16th and 18th centuries, and made a major contribution to the subsequent growth of London as the largest city in the world. The Port of London became the world's busiest, and was the focal point of Empire trade. Today, it is a major financial centre, attracting over 550 foreign banks (the highest concentration in any one place in the world).[1] The London foreign exchange market constitutes over 30% of world turnover – more than New York and Tokyo combined. It is the largest international insurance market and the global market leader in aviation and marine insurance.[2] The City is the marketmaker for the price of bullion and non-ferrous metals, not to mention internationally-traded crude oils. In recent years it has been well placed to take advantage of twenty-four hour trading, given the proximity of the Greenwich meridian. This has contributed significantly to the multi-national and multilingual population of London and created a cosmopolitan working environment.[3]

2. The historical context

London always has been a centre for multiple international trade, as may be seen from City street names such as Old Jewry and Lombard Street (not to mention Little Britain). The Lombards brought foreign banking to England in the Middle Ages, and in their turn City livery companies put up the capital to trade with the remoter parts of the known world through the Muscovy Company on the one hand (1553) and the East India Company on the other (1600).[4] The livery companies tended to be less receptive to incoming trade, however, which they attempted to block through monopolies and by buying commercial protection from the Crown in return for financial support, a system which had come to an end by the 16th century when the Mercers' cartel in silks and fine fabric was successfully broken by foreign competition. The

---

XIII (The role of London as an international financial centre). More recently, the Economic Development Unit has produced a number of research reports which could be of interest:

City skills audit (1998)

The City fringe regeneration audit (1999)

The City's importance to the EU economy (1999)

Contact <edu@corpoflondon.gov.uk> for further inform-ation.

[4] Not that their investment skills or political judgement were always spot on: £50,000 was lost in the Plantation of Ulster, and no fewer than 56 livery companies invested in the first disastrous settlement of Virginia in the early 17th Century. See George Webb's masterful lecture on the livery companies in the City Institutions cycle, delivered at Gresham College in November 1995. (Call 020 7831 0575 for copies.)

---

[1] Over 50% of UK banking assets (£2600bn) are handled by foreign banks, mainly on behalf of foreign customers. See the British Invisibles homepage from the Corporation of London's website at <www.corpoflondon.gov.uk>.

[2] Market share of 23% is double that of its closest competitor, Japan. See website above.

[3] The City Research Project (1993–1994) reported on a variety of themes with an international slant such as number VIII (Debate on international capital requirements), number XII (International banking development and London's position as an international centre) and number

Huguenots, fleeing persecution from France, brought skills in weaving but they also provided commercial skills, as may be seen by the number of Huguenot names that appear in banking – seven out of twenty-four founder directors of the Bank of England in 1694 have Huguenot or Walloon names (Merriman 1993: 14).[5] Joseph Addison, writing in *The Spectator* (which he founded) in the early 18th century, says:

> There is no place in the town I so love to frequent as the Royal Exchange. It gives me a secret satisfaction and in some measure gratifies my vanity as I am an Englishman, to see so rich an assembly of countrymen and foreigners consulting together upon the private business of mankind, and making this metropolis a kind of emporium for the whole earth... I have often been pleased to hear disputes adjusted between an inhabitant of Japan and an Alderman of London; or to see a subject of the Great Mogul entering into a league with one of the Czar of Muscovy. I am infinitely delighted in mixing with these several ministers of commerce, as they are distinguished by their different walks and different languages...
>
> (*The Spectator*, no. 69, 1711)

The Reverend Henry Mayhew produced his celebrated *London Labour and the London Poor*, in four volumes between 1851 and 1862,[6] and with many illustrations of which two are reproduced here.[7]

DOCTOR BOKANKY THE STREET HERBALIST

THE IRISH STREET-SELLER

Sometimes the presence of skilled workers provoked a negative response: the number of German clerks in the Square Mile in the latter part of the 19th century was the subject of a leader in the *Times*:

> It is almost universal testimony that foreigners, especially Germans, are employed in this country to do work which Englishmen ought to perform, and would be employed to perform if they were properly educated.

That was in 1887, the year in which the London Chamber of Commerce also noted that 35% of leading City firms actually employed foreigners (Kynaston 1995:34).[8] Not only were English clerks less proficient linguistically; it was also known that the Germans would work for a lower salary in order to secure commercial experience and a "proper London training", not unlike the Continental students today who are prepared to work as unpaid *stagiaires* as part of their Higher Education.

Mayhew's monumental snapshot of street life over a decade doubtless inspired others, of which Charles Booth's *Life and Labour of the People in London* is the most comprehensive. It was produced between 1889 and 1903 in three sets: (a) the four-volume *Poverty* series (b) the *Industry* series in five volumes, and (c) the *Religious Influences* series in seven volumes, which cover religious life and other activities in different parts of London. The Booth Inquiry includes a series of coloured thematic maps reproduced in Steele (1997). *The Descriptive Map of Poverty* was revised in 1897-98, drawing on information from school board visitors and local police officers.[9] This was followed up by *The New Survey of London Life and Labour* (Anon. 1930) in nine

---

[5] Spitalfields was a major centre for Huguenot refugees.

[6] Volume IV is substantially different from the others in that it lists such things as "The Agencies at present in operation within the Metropolis for the suppression of vice and crime", and includes a lengthy section on prostitution around the world as well as London-based interviews with prostitutes, thieves and swindlers, and beggars. There is also a set of maps and tables.

[7] Thanks for these and other illustrations in this article are due to Jeremy Smith in the Prints and Maps Room at the Guildhall Library for his advice on cuttings and ephemera held in the Noble Collection, and to Irene Gilchrist, Principal Reference Librarian, for her help with references.

[8] This was at a time when the Cavendish Committee was set up to improve Britain's scientific ranking, and County Schools established to raise the educational standards of school-leavers.

[9] The 392 original notebooks are kept in the Booth inquiry Archive at the London School of Economics.

volumes, the first of which assesses the forty years of change since Booth reported. The other volumes assess industry, life and leisure and social surveys by geographical area.

3. Languages and London

The City today is a multi-national and multi-cultural centre, located at the heart of a major world metropolis, for though London may not be the largest city in the world, it is still remarkably diverse, having a long-established cosmopolitan population with everything on offer in a multi-cultural context from special restaurants through to exhibitions and displays of culture. This is not a recent phenomenon, as may be seen by the mosque in the East End which was previously a synagogue, and originally a church,[10] a phenomenon which is merely indicative of the progressive waves of arrivals down the centuries. They have been assimilated into London life within a few generations, bringing skills with them that have added to the wealth and complexity of the capital, ranging from the Flemish weavers who were invited over in 1377 to upgrade the nation's textile industry, to the Huguenots of the 17th and 18th centuries with their knowledge of the silk trade, to the Jewish refugees from mainland Europe who have given their names to respected City firms.[11]

This process of intake and assimilation also means that London offers a peculiar advantage to international firms, namely that staff can be employed with native speaker skills in virtually any world language. London First reports that an increasing number of international firms give as a reason for re-locating to London the fact that they can recruit staff with any range of language skills, an increasing number of whom are bilingual in English and have UK university qualifications (*Evening Standard*, 31 March 1999).

4. Language education and training

(a) The adult learner voucher scheme

A voucher scheme for adult learners was introduced by the Education Committee of the City Corporation in 1993. It provided City residents with a voucher to use (by arrangement) in the learning institution of their choice. The scheme was extended after a pilot phase in 1996 to cover the City's workforce and was designed to involve the employer as well as the worker and the Corporation, in that all three are expected to contribute to the cost of a course. Voucher schemes are by no means unique in educational provision, though they were more strongly favoured by the last Government than the present one. In the case of the City of London they have certain advantages in pinpointing the type of person who should benefit, and are effective in attracting adults on a post-experience part-time basis. The voucher scheme is viewed as a success,

although it has taken longer to reach the anticipated levels of take-up than had originally been hoped. But the pattern of use among residents has been encouraging within the context of government policy concerning lifelong learning and widened access as the vouchers have had a trigger effect in drawing people into education courses who were not regular users before.

It is not surprising that language courses have been of particular interest. Figures for learning vouchers in 1998–99 indicate that languages constitute the largest area for choice of subject: 36%, with the broader "business and professional category" following at 25.6%. Curiously enough, information technology figures at the bottom of the list at only 8.8%.[12] This is in contrast to the findings of the skills audit commissioned by the City Corporation in 1998, where IT was seen as the biggest problem area for recruitment (26% of the survey).[13] This does not tally with our experience at City University, where information technology courses comprise around 30% of part-time evening enrolments, with languages in second place at 21%. The emphasis on languages in the Corporation's voucher scheme is commented on in the evaluation (Jarvis 1997:56). It is seen as some-thing that fits well into a programme of life-long learning as one of the most applicable of those skills which are vocationally relevant but which do not require a specialist background or even previous knowledge. Increasingly people in London now have previous experience of studying a language, so the subject is seen as being non-threatening, and there are obvious personal advantages in terms of travel and tourism. The benefits to language learning in particular are noted in the survey, echoing the *Times* leader of 1887 (referred to above):

> The salaries of clerks are only prevented from falling by the addition of fresh branches of knowledge which were not, but are now, exacted. Few among the new generation of clerks have not added shorthand, and at least one language to their qualifications.

(b) Types of provision

It is difficult to quantify the amount of in-house training. Small-group activity is commonplace, running for up to three months at a time, usually during the lunch-hour once or twice a week. This is sometimes paid for by the participants themselves. Regular lunchtime classes are offered by the two universities: London Guildhall University at its Moorgate site and the City University activity, housed at the Bishopsgate Institute which happens to be adjacent to the Broadgate and Spitalfields developments, which are both fairly recent and provide large concentrations of City workers (23,000 in the former and 11,000 in the latter).[14]

---

[10]   In Brick Lane. It was originally a Huguenot church.

[11]   See David Kynaston's (1994-99) monumental history of the City of London, vol. II in particular.

---

[12]   Internal Corporation report (ref. 224AEPF, 17 June 1999). See also Jarvis (1997:38).

[13]   The City skills audit (1998), page 16 (see note 3 above).

[14]   The Bishopsgate Foundation was established in 1894, with funding drawn from old parish charities. It has a public library, a new and vibrant range of courses aimed at City workers, and a broader charitable role. It is located almost opposite Liverpool Street station at 230 Bishopsgate.

It is curious that there is not more demand for work-related language courses. But this may be put down to the fact that most students who enrol in group classes are looking for the development of the language skill as a whole, with emphasis on social skills and travel situations. People are also interested in current affairs and want access to the foreign-language press or (increasingly) satellite television and the internet. But in the multi-national companies, and even in the ones which are foreign or part foreign-owned, English is the standard language for everyday communication. Staff who need to operate in the target language tend to be employed with that skill in place, or are quite possibly native speakers, as mentioned above. In addition, it is apparent that where companies see a need for a high-level language skill then they will pay large sums for intensive executive-style one-to-one training through well-known providers or send the individual abroad for a similar immersion course.[15]

The current take-up rate for language classes is strong (with Spanish and Italian currently in prime position) and language tutors report a high level of motivation among students. (None so high as the person who rang the University to enquire about language classes in September, and said that he wanted to be bilingual by Christmas...). However, it must be said that traditionally there is a high drop-out rate from adult language classes. It is a common pattern for a class to recruit 20 in the autumn term, for 12 to enrol in spring and 8 to carry on into the summer. This situation is monitored regularly: the normal reasons given for non-continuation are pressures of work (including overseas travel at short notice); family problems and personal health.

(c) Styles of learning

The growth of different styles of learning fitted to individual needs, coupled with the development of multi-media and the infinite horizons offered by the Internet, provide a new range of challenges to the linguists and also offer a more flexible solution to individual learning needs. A significant number of people are unable to commit themselves to regular classes. Long hours are common in the Square Mile to allow for opening and closing times in Hong Kong and New York. It is not surprising, therefore, that both providers and clients look to different modes of course delivery.[16]

There are, however, still obstacles to be faced. Employers discourage staff from using their PCs for what are seen as unofficial purposes, which is understandable in terms of cost, lost time and dangers of viruses, cookies and trojans. However, the desktop PC constitutes a major learning resource, and it is to be hoped that a way can be found to exploit it to the full.[17] Ironically, the use of the PC would go some way to resolving the problems of time and space that so often arise when looking at in-company training. Company policy has a key role to play here, as well as government initiatives such as the new University for Industry. However, training costs have to be found from within constrained budgets, and at times there will be conflicting needs between, for example, seminars on new tax legislation and ongoing areas of training such as IT and languages. (Of the three areas mentioned, languages are likely to take the lowest priority, but will also probably be the least expensive!)

(d) The London Market Language Exchange

An interesting experiment has been developed around the insurance and re-insurance industry. There is an active range of language clubs which have been developed in recent years for members of Lloyd's and the International Underwriting Association (IUA). They are independent and freestanding, provide opportunities for language learning and teaching and are active socially. They have received support from the City Corporation in recent years, which provides for coordination and some teaching.[18] Seven languages are now involved (French, German, Italian, Japanese, Portuguese, Russian and Spanish). There are interesting links abroad, principally with ENASS (the Ecole National d'Assurance in Paris), and El Instituto Mapfre in Madrid. Talks have also been held with the Verein de Deutschen Versicherungs Fachwirte in Cologne with a view to strengthening international links.

In 1998 the City Corporation provided funding for City University to develop a web-support page on behalf of the clubs (which use the umbrella name London Market Language Exchange, LMLE, using the IUA website). It is designed to be easily accessible to the 350 members, many of whom travel, quite possibly at short notice. It provides a newsletter, information about the club officers, a list of useful websites related to the language and country concerned, and links across to other websites, such as the electronic newspaper which is run by City University students (those from Journalism provide the stories and the ones from Informatics put them on the Web).[19] Business School undergraduates at City University are being linked with students at ENASS from Autumn 1999 as an on-line learning experiment. There is an enormous amount of material that can be used in cyberspace, but a number of practical difficulties arise for the individual learner: websites change addresses with some frequency, many are not as effective as they claim to be; some are not easy to move around in. A range of annotated websites under the headings of reference works, country information, language

15   The Nuffield Foundation is conducting an inquiry into current learning provision, needs and trends. See Moys (1998).

16   City University offers a distance scheme for business languages, aimed principally at MBA students who want to include a language in a timetable which typically runs from 9 till 6 on three days a week, with two days clear for project work. A full description of the language activity at City University is to be found on the homepage at <www.city.ac.uk/languages>.

17   Misuse of the PC can lead to disciplinary action and even dismissal. See the *Independent*, 28 June 1999, and the *Daily Mail*, 16 June 1999. But then a survey carried out by Infosecurity, SC Magazine and NetPartners calculated that companies a losing £2500 of staff time per year as employees search for new jobs, check out sports results and visit "adult" sites (*Daily Mail* 10 August 1999).

18   The club coordinator is Martin Reiss who may be contacted c/o GAN Insurance Co. Ltd, Suite 4a, Lower Ground Floor, London Underwriting Centre, 3 Minster Court, Mincing Lane, London EC3R 7DD; <martin.reiss@yahoo.com>

19   SENAC is available at <www.city.ac.uk/linguanews>.

learning and miscellany is being developed on the City University language website with a link across to the LMLE club pages.

5. From the single market to the millennium

In 1992 the City Corporation commissioned a survey – jointly with the Bank of England – of language skills and needs of City firms. 67 companies took part,[20] and 90% expected to conduct "significant business" with or in the non-English speaking world. Of these, 76% expected language skills to contribute significantly to competitiveness. Yet only about half had a policy on language skills and training. Of difficulties encountered, the following were listed by up to half of the survey: conflicts of time, lack of suitable training and shortage of funds. "Solutions" proposed included larger budgets; more business-orientated language training; better quality of training; and more out-of-hours provision. Validation of courses and appropriate certification were also considered important. A number of respondents hoped to avoid language problems by recruiting suitably qualified staff.

The questions on likely future needs and levels of provision make interesting reading in the light of the changes that have occurred in the past six years. Globalisation has become a commonplace word, and the international element of the Square Mile has become stronger through mergers and acquisitions. It is therefore interesting to compare the responses in 1992 with a survey of members of the LMLE, taken in August and September 1999, which is indicative of the current position of language skills and training issues in at least one key City sector. 90 questionnaires were received from a total of 350 language club members (see Appendix 1). Predictably, French is the language most in evidence, with 20% of respondents claiming to be fluent, followed by 9% for German and 6% for Spanish. The token numbers present in Dutch, Italian, Polish and Swedish are made up of native speakers. (Just under 10% of those who responded were non-native speakers of English.) French does not figure as strongly as German among those who claim to speak a language well (5%, versus 22%). Portuguese and Italian figure just above Polish, Russian and Spanish, which each have one adherent, plus (curiously enough) one for Yiddish. Average competence is claimed by most people again in French (26%), followed as usual by German (14%). Italian appears more strongly at this point (9%), significantly ahead of Spanish and Russian (both just below 3%). Portuguese is joined by Hebrew this time and, intriguingly, Haitian (presumably Creole French). French comes to the fore through all those rusty O-levels (42%), with German way below at 14% and Italian and Spanish level-pegging at 7%. Arabic, Hebrew, Latin, Polish, Russian and Serbo-Croat just get a mention.

The emphasis on the conventional Western European languages accounts for the high number of respondents who put School down as their source of

learning (92%). University (24%) probably reflects the number of actual language graduates in the survey rather than the total number of people holding a degree (though it may include people who took a language as voluntary or subsidiary option within a different discipline). 17%, however, claim to have acquired their language skills at home. This reflects the number of native speakers in the survey, and there is no distinction between those having bilingual parentage and those who have acquired a language through marriage. Previous surveys have indicated that, when questioned about language skills, respondents assume that the question deals with the languages of education rather than a home or "heritage" language,[21] and so the lack of data in response to this question does not necessarily indicate that there is a lack of more widely-spoken world languages in the workplace. It should also be borne in mind that this survey has focused on members of the language clubs so that they are not necessarily representative of the workforce as a whole. It is perhaps significant that in response to Question 12 of the original Bank of England survey (which asked companies to provide a breakdown of the total number of staff with language skills of varying fluency) very few companies had that data to hand, or only had data on "relevant" languages, such as Japanese in the case of a Japanese bank. And in any case the level of language skill at the time did not seem to be as high as companies might have wished. LMLE members are perhaps self-selecting in that their membership of a language club is indicative of their personal interests. However, 52% report that the need for language skills has risen since the advent of the Single Market in 1992, while only 4% feel that it has gone down (and that may be because of particular factors in their own job). 38%, on the other hand, felt that the situation was unchanged, which may reflect the international element of the world's insurance markets rather than any wish not to view their work from a wider global perspective. More specifically, 57% of those surveyed draw most on reading skills in a foreign language as part of their work; 22% need to write (which suggests that e-mails are done in English, which reflects the current position of English rather than any other language on the Web, although that situation is changing),[22] 66% find themselves speaking a foreign language, which points to telephone work, but intriguingly only 36% say that they draw on listening skills, which suggests that some of those telephone conversations are rather one-sided.

The language clubs are designated as such because members do not just go to classes as part of their activities. Much of their language learning takes place in a social context, and people also upgrade the linguistic skills by learning informally from each other, although trained teachers are provided (with support from the City Corporation) for classes at beginners and lower intermediate levels. Even so, the clubs are not just made up of people compensating

---

[20] Community education, foreign language skills survey and other related matters. Education Committee minutes EDU 9.93, dated 18 January 1993, agenda item 8f.

[21] In LEA usage, 'heritage language' refers to a language other than English spoken by the child's immediate family. such as parents or grandparents.

[22] Graddol (1997:50) acknowledges that 80% of e-mail traffic is in English, but points out that 90% of computers are currently located in English-speaking countries.

for a lack of previous language skills. Only 28% have started a new language in the past five years, most of those being speakers of French hoovering up a second Romance language – Spanish, Italian or Portuguese, in that order, though Russian also figures. Polish is the only other Eastern European language mentioned. It is possible, though, that people use German as a lingua franca in their dealings with that part of the world. 31% have seen fit to revive a language that they once spoke better and this (inevitably, given its predominance in the school curriculum) is French. That is put in some sort of context by the student who writes, "I was taught Latin and Classical Greek at school but have forgotten just about everything. Of course, this has been a huge help with all other languages." (Quite.)

Given the cyclic nature of work in the insurance industry and the enormous pressures on time at certain periods of the year, it is heartening to see that people are prepared to dedicate quite a lot of their spare time to language study or, in this context, at least the social activities that go with it! The extremes are not strongly represented: 6% spend less than 3 hours a month while 9% give 10 hours more. 40% spend between 4 and 7 hours which tallies with the common practice of taking a two-hour evening class on a regular basis.

Less encouraging is the response to the question about company policy on language training. 52% say that there isn't one, though a lot of people qualify that statement by adding that they are not aware of one, or are not sure what the policy or procedures are. Of the 21% who do reply in the affirmative, the following points seem to apply: staff with a clear training need are sent on specific courses, or in-house training is provided (pre-sumably on a one-to-one basis) and time off is given to attend examinations (though not, it would appear, to revise for them). Learning materials, such as CD-ROMs, are also available in some cases. Staff who go on language courses that might be relevant to work have their fees paid; staff are encouraged to go to the language club activities. It is also noted that job advertisements, for large companies in particular, make specific reference to language skills, but that employers tend not to make maximum potential use of such skills among their staff. (One language student outside this survey has commented that a knowledge of a key language can actually inhibit mobility within the workplace because of a lack of other staff capable of taking over the work.) Languages were seen in one case as being helpful in widening the opportunities for job development and interaction within existing jobs, only employers tend to take a reactive view and turn to language training to meet a specific require-ment (such as the need to travel abroad) rather than view it as part of a wider global strategy. The initiative would appear to come from students who want to acquire or improve a language, rather than from line managers or training officers who see language acquisition as part of career or company development. One questionnaire raises the appro-priateness of the type of language courses normally available, given the highly technical terminology which may be needed, and the fact that the usage of related terms can differ between languages. One student has actually produced a glossary of such terms in more than one language, an initiative that could be of benefit to a wider number of people.

6. Concluding points

Continued research into language skills and provision for learning will surely demonstrate the benefits accruing to the City of London of the cosmopolitan, multilingual and multicultural population upon which it can draw for its workers at all levels. For international firms, this can offer the prospect of insights into the society behind virtually any world market, and the prospect of using staff who can not only communicate with any of those markets but also have some understanding as to how they function and why. Those firms have the added confidence of knowing that those employees bring with them qualifications arising from their education in this country, which are known and recognised. In turn there is a challenge for the education providers, who train those staff in the first place, to ensure that they are not only proud of their particular heritage but also see that there are distinct commercial advantages to be had in improving the skills that they have got and applying them within the context of their chosen profession or occupation. Nor should it be assumed that the language issue can be postponed in some way or does not need to be addressed. Machine translation is making strides, but is nowhere near perfection, and machine interpreting of anything more than what could have been sent down a telex machine ten years ago is a long way off. And even an organisation with as vested an interest in the continued supremacy of English as the British Council is concerned that in the next 50 years the world situation could change to give prominence to a range of other languages: some predictable (Arabic, Chinese, Hindi/Urdu), others less so, such as Malay. In any case, Spanish and Russian are the only European languages that figure; Spanish given its pre-eminence in the Americas, and Russian because of the potential growth in trade blocs, which may well drive the trends towards the most useful (rather than the most widely spoken) languages worldwide. English is, however, set most likely to continue as the world's lingua franca, but that will not necessarily help when gathering market intelligence or when dealing on the ground in target markets (Graddol 1998:58). And of the ten largest cities in the world today, none are in Europe and only two (New York and Los Angeles) are in an English-speaking country, although arguably Bombay and Calcutta could be added.

There is also the challenge of ensuring that the world's premier financial centre can maintain its position as a world focus for higher education and be recognised as a key location for financial education in particular. For the City Corporation there is the task of building links and contacts with the fringe and outer boroughs to ensure that the wealth of human potential can be realised, and that the cycles of relative poverty and deprivation must be tackled for good reasons at all levels.[23] And

---

[23] For further details on partnerships (both existing and planned) with neighbouring boroughs, contact:

research still needs to be conducted into the skills base which is present, combining a knowledge of a language that goes beyond the conventional Western European ones with marketable skills.[24] There is scope for development also through the Corporation's own Business Traineeship Programmes. It should not be forgotten either that the Declaration of Human Rights comes into law from January 2000, which will have a wide range of implications for the provision of language services and support in legal, health and local government situations, the full implications of which have yet to be grasped. A recent report by the Institute of Linguists, for example, drew attention to the language problems that face the emergency services should they ever be faced with a major incident (such as a plane crash) if numbers of non-native speakers of English are involved.[25] The Corporation also needs to persuade City firms of the linguistic assets that they have to hand, as it is to the benefit of all if London maintains its pre-eminence as the foremost international trading centre. Perhaps Mrs Aphra Behn was right when she said more than 300 years ago, "Money speaks sense in a language all nations understand".[26] Perhaps so, but having the world at its fingertips while standing on the Greenwich Meridian surely places the City of London in a unique position. It would be tragic if such an advantage were to be wasted.[27]

Professor Tim Connell is at City University where he holds a personal chair in Languages for the Professions. He has a particular interest in translator and interpreter training, which has brought him into contact with a wide range of linguistic communities in London.

Bibliography

Anon. 1930-35 *The New Survey of London Life & Labour* (1930-1935), London: P S King.

Behn, Aphra 1677 *The Rover*. London: John Amery.

Besant, Walter 1903 *East London*. London: Chatto & Windus, 2nd edition (1st edition: 1901).

Canning, J. (ed.) 1986 *The illustrated Mayhew's London*. London: Guild Publishing.

Doolittle, Ian G 1982 *The City of London and its livery companies*, Dorchester: Gavin Press.

Graddol, David 1997 *The future of English?* London: The British Council.

Jarvis, Peter et al. 1997 *Towards the learning city*. London: Corporation of London.

Kennedy Malling, John 1988 *Discovering London's guilds and liveries*. Aylesbury: Shire. [This contains interesting information on the guilds in European countries.]

Kynaston, David 1994–99 *The City of London*. London: Chatto & Windus, 4 vols.

McAuley, Ian 1993 *Guide to ethnic London*. London: Immel, 2nd edition (1st edition: London: Haag, 1987). [Also a Carlton TV series.]

Mayhew, Henry 1851 *London labour and the London poor; a cyclopaedia of the conditions and earnings of those that will work, those than cannot work, and those that will not work*. London, 3 vols. [See Quennell (ed.) below for more recent, annotated editions of this work with a range of contemporary illustrations.]

Merriman, Nick (ed.) 1993 *The peopling of London: fifteen hundred years of settlement from overseas*. London: Museum of London.

Moys, Alan (ed.) 1998 *Where are we going with languages?* London: Nuffield Foundation.

Quennell, Peter (ed.) 1949 *Mayhew's London*. London: Pilot Press.

—— 1950 *Mayhew's underworld*. London: William Kimber.

—— 1951 *Mayhew's characters*. London: William Kimber. [Another edition of this volume was published by Spring Books in 1961, and includes the following interviews which deal with foreign characters: 'The street-seller of rhubarb and spice' (Moroccan); 'The Gun-exercise exhibitor – one-legged Italian'; 'Italian pipers and clarionet players'; 'An Italian with monkey'.]

Steele, J (ed.) 1997 *The streets of London: the Booth notebooks*. London: Deptford Forum.

Weinreb, Ben & Hibbert, Christopher 1983 *The London encyclopaedia*. London: Macmillan.

<jennifer.cook@corpoflondon.gov.uk>.

[24] The 1991 census, for example, does not collect data on language backgrounds – other than for Welsh and Gaelic.

[25] *The Linguist* vol. 38, no. 5, pp 130-34.

[26] Act III, scene I of her play entitled *The Rover* (1677).

[27] Thanks are due to many people in the City who have contributed to this study, in particular the Assistant Education Officer at the City Corporation, Stephen Denny; Penny Rawlins at the Economic Development Unit; Martin Reiss and colleagues at IUA; and to Lori-Ann Scott of London Guildhall University who collated all the LMLE data.

Appendix 1

Questionnaire for the London Markets Language Exchange

Name:

Organisation:

Telephone number:

e-mail:

1) How many languages do you speak?

    Fluently Well   Average   Slightly

a)

b)

c)

2) Do you use any of your languages as part of your daily routine? If so, which ones?

3) Has the demand for language skills in your working life changed since 1992?

a) Up __   b) Down __   c) Unchanged __

4) Which skills do you draw on most:

(a) Reading   (b) Writing

(c) Speaking   (d) Listening

5) Where do your languages "come from"?

(a) School

(b) University

(c) Home

(d) Previous work experience

(e) Personal interest

6) Have you learnt a new language in the past five years?

7) Have you revived a language that you once spoke better?

8) How much time do you spend on language study per month?

9) Does your company have a policy on language training?

      THANK YOU FOR YOUR CO-OPERATION.
      PLEASE ADD ANY COMMENTS BELOW:

Appendix 2

Places of worship within (or just outside) the City with services in languages other than English

The Christian church obviously has a cosmopolitan history. The first church of St Paul in London was founded by an Italian bishop in 604 AD; in 1550 the Strangers' Church was founded at the Austin Friars in 1550, with Dutch, German and French people in the congregation. A synagogue was established in Creechurch Lane in 1656 and a Greek Orthodox church in St Giles in 1677 (Merriman 1993:210).

A little-known linguistic feature of the City today is the range of Church services that take place during a month in languages ranging from Amharic to Welsh:

Dutch Church, 7 Austin Friars.   *Dutch* (Ecumenical)

St Andrew's by the Wardrobe, Queen Victoria St.
                    Malayalam (Indian Orthodox)

St Anne and St Agnes, Gresham Street.
                      German (Lutheran)

(This church also holds services in *Estonian*, *Latvian* and *Swahili*)

St Benet, Queen Street.   *Welsh*

St Botolph without Bishopsgate, Bishopsgate.
                          Japanese

St Dunstan in the West, Fleet Street.
            Romanian Orthodox (Patriarchal)

St Vedast alias Foster, Cheapside.   *Amharic*

In addition, St Etheldreda's in Ely Place still has a sung Latin Mass.

For further information, see the Friends of the City Churches website at: <www.london-city-churches.org>.

Just outside the Square Mile there is St Boniface (German Roman Catholic) in Adler Street, E1, and also St Peter's Italian Church in Clerkenwell Road, EC1.

Among a number of mosques situated just outside the City, the largest is the East London Mosque Trust Ltd, 82-92 Whitechapel Road, E1.

Several synagogues serve the City, including the Bevis Marks Synagogue, Bevis Marks, EC3 and the Sandys Row Synagogue, Middlesex Street, E1.

Ethnic and linguistic diversity:
the impact on local authority expenditure

Jo Mennell

The population of London is unique in terms of the extent and the diversity of its characteristics. These social, demographic and geographic variations have a significant impact both on the need to provide services and the cost of those services. Ethnic and linguistic diversity make their own very specific demands on local authority service provision and it is important that these are fully identified to ensure that authorities are adequately resourced to meet the needs of the different minority ethnic communities in London.

In order to put the impact of specific service needs on local authority budgets into context, it is useful to have some understanding of the background to the local government distribution system.

Local Government Finance – A brief introduction

The Revenue Support Grant

The distribution of resources to local authorities is an area that is guaranteed to engender strongly-held opinion in the local government world. The most hotly contested area is the distribution of revenue funding through a series of formulae known as standard spending assessments (SSAs). These are divided into major service blocks, such as education, social services, police, fire, highways maintenance, and environmental, protective and cultural services. These distribute financial support from central government to cover revenue expenditure. These include day-to-day costs such as salaries and wages, heating, lighting, transport, insurance and other routine expenditure necessary to provide services. Other longer-term costs such as building costs and repairs are generally termed capital expenditure.

Each local authority in England annually receives Revenue Support Grant (RSG) from central government. In addition to this, authorities receive specific and special grants and funding from the national business rate pool. The difference between what an authority receives in its grant and its actual budget is the amount it has to raise from council tax.

Why is the amount of Revenue Support Grant so important to local authorities?

There are two main reasons why the distribution of revenue resources is controversial. First, there is the issue of quantum of resources. There is a widely held view in local government that the size of the total pot of resources distributed to local authorities in England is inadequate, especially when compared to the amount distributed to Scotland, Wales and Northern Ireland. In consequence, the issue of distribution is given much greater prominence than would otherwise be the case.

Second, the amount of financial support received from central grant is vitally important because local authorities are limited in the amount and overall percentage of their resources they can raise locally from the council tax. In recent years the balance of funding has shifted away from locally collected resources from local council taxpayers and businesses and it is now heavily dependent on central government grant. In 1989–90, the balance of funding between central government grant and locally collected funding was as follows:

	Total standard spending	% funded by central government grant	% funded by local funding
1989-90	£31.5 bn	43.2%	56.8%

Under this system, changes in central government grant did not have the far-reaching impact they do at present because losses could be offset, in part or in full, by some increase in the total amount raised locally. However, following the introduction of the National Non-Domestic Rate (NNDR) and the centralisation of the business rates in April 1990, the balance shifted dramatically.

	Total standard spending	% funded by central government grant	% funded by local funding
1990–91	£32.8 bn	70.4%	29.6%
1999–2000	£50.6 bn	78.1%	21.9%

From 1990, authorities were no longer responsible for setting their own business rate poundage. One national multiplier replaced these, and revenue collected from the business rate pool was now paid into a national pool. Although NNDR is redistributed from the national pool to authorities on the basis of their resident populations, the introduction of the NNDR directly resulted in a shift in the balance to a greater dependency and emphasis on central government grant. This happens where authorities have a small local tax base relative to their spending needs. This is clearly illustrated in the London borough of Tower Hamlets. Local deprivation means it has high spending needs but it also has a relatively small tax base. The combination of these factors mean that a 1% reduction in its standard spending assessment would mean a 9% increase in council tax.

The Languages of London project and its significance for local government funding

This grant dependency culture means that changes to the distribution formula can have a disproportionate impact on the level of council tax and the extent and quality of services provided. It is therefore no surprise that authorities take a keen and active interest in discussions about data and methodology. Authorities, often at opposite ends of the political spectrum, are drawn together to argue their position on sparsity of population, deprivation, wage costs etc. Until the recently announced government review of revenue grant distribution resulted in a moratorium on changes to the distribution mechanism, the annual negotiations frequently involved in excess of 100 technical papers.

81

The major problem for London in terms of negotiating a fair local government finance distribution is ensuring that any formula reflects its unique and diverse characteristics. This is particularly true of its cultural and ethnic diversity and the specific service needs they generate. The success of the government's dispersal policy for asylum seekers and the generation of new communities of refugees in the regions will also have a profound effect on the requirement of local government to support diverse communities.

The MacPherson report into the murder of Stephen Lawrence emphasises the value of appropriate services for black and ethnic groups. Also, the forthcoming Local Government Bill is expected to contain an additional duty for local government to enhance and secure the economic, social and environmental wellbeing of their areas will emphasise the importance of appropriate services.

By highlighting the extent of linguistic diversity, the Languages of London project raises awareness of the additional demands on service delivery in a multicultural environment. Research, which provides a better understanding of these issues, is particularly important to London local government.

Current funding

The Ethnic Minority Achievement Grant (EMAG) was recently introduced for 1999–2000 to replace the education element of the Section 11 grant.[1] This funding is intended to help provide equality of opportunity for all minority ethnic groups. It aims to be more targeted than its predecessor by including additional groups that Section 11 failed to fund. However, EMAG funding is cash-limited and its impact is restricted by (i) the size of the total of available resources, and (ii) the need for authorities to find additional funding to supplement their allocation. Although the grant has been in operation for only a short time, authorities are already experiencing considerable difficulties in meeting the match funded element. This is particularly the case for those authorities with high numbers of refugee and asylum-seeking pupils.

Similarly, the government provides special grants for services to destitute asylum seekers and is expected to make funds available for the settlement of refugees following the passage of the Immigration and Asylum Bill. However, the special grants received by London authorities currently only reimburse a proportion of actual expenditure.

Therefore, it is important that the revenue distribution system (SSAs) also targets ethnic diversity.

The standard spending assessment system is widely expected to identify the service needs of different client groups and any additional demands they might have. The Association of London Government believes that it is imperative that the distribution of resources is able to identify the linguistic and other challenges faced by local authorities with diverse ethnic populations. Currently, these needs are not fully identified. For example, the existing measure of ethnicity is a census–based one and is general in definition. It does not target the new minority ethnic groups as effectively as one would expect a distribution indicator to do. However, while data refinements are clearly desirable, we must not lose sight of the underlying importance of including some measure of ethnicity/linguistic allegiance in any formula which distributes revenue resources to local authorities.

In recent years the Association of London Government has been forced to defend London's position on additional resources to meet the needs of its minority ethnic population. Ethnicity was removed from the Children's Personal Social Services formula for 1999–2000 in spite of evidence that there is a foster and adoptive carer shortage for children from minority ethnic backgrounds and as a consequence they spend longer in residential care.

There has been pressure from authorities outside London to remove the ethnicity indicator from the education formulae. The Association is firmly opposed to this. We believe that being able to identify new minority ethnic groups is a key factor in distributing resources because there is a much greater need to spend where, for example, children have English as a second language. The Languages of London study shows that many education authorities in London have to respond to the additional needs of children from many different cultural and ethnic backgrounds. Children attending schools in London speak more than 300 different languages. This creates additional challenges for schools in the capital and has resource implications. If these children are to be given the same opportunities as those with English as a first language, we have a collective responsibility to continue to refine the data that identify their needs.

Jo Mennell is the Senior Government Finance Officer of the Association of London Government (ALG). The ALG represents the interests of all 33 London councils and the London Fire and Civil Defence Authority. It provides member authorities with a single voice in negotiations with central government to ensure that London gets its fair share of resources. The ALG is consulted formally by the Government, and is in an ideal position to advise on a wide range of issues relating to local government and other matters of concern to Londoners. It also works closely with many private, voluntary and public sector bodies.

Enquiries about the ALG may be sent by e-mail to <jmennell@alg.gov.uk>.

---

[1] For more about this, as well as the history of the Section 11 grant, see John Eversley's article (*this volume*, pp 61-62).

An indicator for health needs of minority ethnic communities in the capital

Pui-Ling Li

Ethnicity data, collected for the first time in the 1991 census, have been used extensively by government departments as an indicator for needs. It is one of a number of indicators used for weighting the national formulae for the allocation of resources to health and local authorities. However, the ten census categories for ethnicity[1] do not reflect the diversity of communities in this country, and mask the differences of their health needs. Furthermore, the data become less and less meaningful over time as different population groups move in and out of the country, particularly in London.

In the health service, the collection of ethnicity data by general practices is probably the closest we can get to having a geographically-based population denominator for minority ethnic communities which takes account of population movements over time. However, we are a long way from having this systematically collected in a standardized format. Hospitals, on the other hand, have been collecting ethnicity data for hospital inpatient activity but the usefulness of these data is hampered by the variable extent to which it is collected across the country. Furthermore, this only offers one dimension of health needs, that of health service use.

In London, where one in five residents are from black and minority ethnic communities, up-to-date information on ethnicity is of particular importance, both for the assessment of needs and the planning of services. The data collected by London schools on the languages other than English spoken by their children at home may provide a useful proxy for the population distribution and the size of these communities until the next census.

Although there are limitations associated with this information – such as the absence of a standardized format for data recording, the lack of information on the children's fluency in English, the need for teachers to determine the type of languages spoken for very young children which may not always be accurate, and the exclusion of those children who attend private schools – it does offer an indication of the geographical distribution and the size of different Black and minority ethnic communities. Clearly, this information does not offer a measure for those who have no children or no school-aged children, but if we consider the distribution with what we understand about the pattern of immigration and the population structure for each group, it is possible to make some assessment of their needs. Furthermore, the data are collected yearly, and it is thus possible to look at geographical movements of different communities over time.

With a total of 300 different languages being spoken in London, the data demonstrate very clearly the diversity in the Capital's population. But what is of particular interest is the discovery of unexpected pockets of minority ethnic communities – such as Hungarians in Harrow or Armenians in Ealing – in areas previously undetected by the last census. Although the data cannot provide a precise measure of the burden of health needs for each community, the maps which illustrate the distribution of the languages spoke by schoolchildren can be used for pinpointing those geographical areas where particular attention should be focused.

At a pan-London level, this information could be useful for informing the development of the London Health Strategy; the implementation of the national priorities in Saving Lives: Our Healthier Nation; the performance management of commissioners and providers of health and social care; and the implementation of both the NHS and social services performance assessment framework.

At a district and borough level, where inter-agency working is essential if the root causes of ill health and health inequalities are to be tackled effectively, the information can usefully contribute to the cross linking of different over-arching strategies such as the Health Action Zone and Education Action Zone initiatives. It can also provide the focus for joint action between on-going health and social care initiatives such as Single Regeneration Budget, and new programmes such as Sure Start, Quality Protects, and New Deal for Communities.

The information could be used to help identify priorities in the health improvement programme, a strategic framework for the health authority and partner agencies to deliver health gain for a local population. It will not only add to the demographic information of the populations covered by primary care groups, and later, by primary care trusts, but it will also provide the focus for targeting needs assessment, contribute to the planning and commissioning of services, and inform the debate around health inequalities.

From the communities' perspective, this information will be useful for targeting efforts in obtaining funds from the statutory sector for meeting health needs and in working in partnership with statutory agencies. This is of particular importance to dispersed communities such as the Chinese who would benefit from inter-agency working which span district and borough boundaries.

It is also of benefit to statutory agencies to be able to identify appropriate partners for collaboration and the sharing of resources to meet needs. This offers a route into addressing the issues around equity, and a good example would be the development of a pan-London resource for health advocacy so that scarce resources can be used to best effect.

Dr Pui-Ling Li is consultant in public health at the London Region of the National Health Service Executive where she leads work on primary care, mental health, and refugees. She is also part of the team which manages the performance of health authorities and NHS trusts. She was a GP in East London for five years and is Chair of the Chinese National Healthy Living Centre. She may be contacted by e-mail at <pli@doh.gov.uk>.

---

1   The ten categories are: White, Black Caribbean, Black African, Black Other, Indian, Pakistani, Bangladeshi, Chinese, Other Asian, and Other.

84

Coming to school in London from abroad

During the course of preparing this volume, contributors encountered various people born abroad who vividly recalled their feelings when they began attending school in London. Some of these were invited to put their experiences in writing for possible use in this book. While it cannot be claimed that the three reproduced below are in any way representative, we feel they merit inclusion because they suggest an interesting and potentially very valuable area for further research. [Eds]

From Pakistan

I arrived in England from Pakistan in May 1967. I was 5 years old. I don't remember anything of the journey, but I do remember some of my early days at school here.

When we lived in Pakistan my Dad made a great deal of effort to teach me the Urdu alphabet and I remember evenings at home and Dad using a slate and chalk to teach me. In London, in order to teach me English, I was definitely given the short end of the stick. During the morning at infant school I would be expected to join the usual lesson that the children had, with no additional support. However, in the afternoon, when all the other children played, myself and three or four other Asian children (of various ages) would go off to have an English lesson, taught by an Asian woman. I don't remember this phase in my life lasting for very long, I suppose because being surrounded by English speakers all day long I absorbed the language very quickly.

Not speaking English was obviously a challenge but it was not the only thing I had to learn. It seemed that my traditional shalwar and kameez were not suitable wear for school and I remember being taken home by a teacher who was in possession of a yellow dress with white polka dots on it. This, the teacher tried to explain to my mother – who couldn't speak English – is what I should wear to school.

Nazir Moya

From Puerto Rico

I was born in Spain but, at the age of ten, my mother took me and my younger brother to the USA and then to Puerto Rico. We always spoke Spanish at home and most of the time I was in a Spanish-speaking environment. Then, at the age of fifteen, I came to London and was thrown into classes preparing for GCSEs. I'd got quite fluent at English in the USA and Puerto Rico but spoke it with an American accent, which seemed to make a favourable impression on the other schoolkids, so no problem there. But, looking back, the teachers didn't understand that English wasn't my first language and that created problems. I had a really hard time trying to cope with some of the subjects like maths. They thought that, because I could talk in fluent English with the other pupils, I understood everything in English. But I didn't. Many of the words the teachers used in the lessons and in the textbooks we had were entirely new to me. I think the teachers just thought I wasn't very bright. My parents tried to put them right about that, which helped a bit. In the end I got better grades than most of the other pupils – but it was a hard struggle.

Luis Gonzalez

From Fiji

I came to London from Fiji in 1972. I was 12 years old. I spoke Hindi at home with my family. I could also speak Fijian but I knew very little English. I had attended a Hindi-medium school in Fiji.

I remember how excited I felt the first day I went to my new school, a comprehensive in north London. But this feeling did not last long. The head teacher looked through the school records I had brought from Fiji and was unimpressed. He put me in a below average class, perhaps because my English was poor.

I was the only Indian in the class. Apart from three Blacks, all the other pupils were White. I got called all sorts of insulting names. At first, I did not know what the words meant so I just smiled. But I soon knew they were meant to hurt me. And there was bullying and fighting. After one week I hated the place. At one point things got so bad I ran away from school. But that didn't help: I got beaten by my own father and caned when I returned to school.

It took me about a year to become really fluent in English. And only then did I begin to make a few friends. After about two years I began to enjoy school. Some success in sports helped to make me feel part of things. But I never had any success with the subjects taught at school and left without any qualifications when I was 16.

Today I speak and write pretty good English but that is no thanks to school; it is due to the company I have kept since leaving school. Even so, I only have a poorly paid office job. Maybe, if I had come to London when I was two or three years younger, things would have worked out better.

Satish Naidu

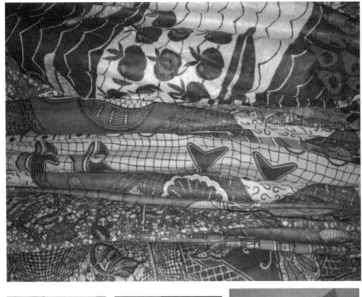

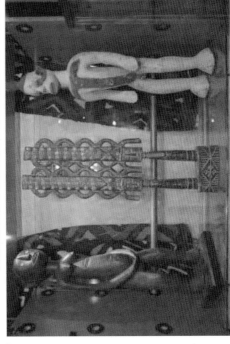

Towards obtaining better data
on the languages of London's schoolchildren

Philip Baker and Antony Sanderson

Designing a questionnaire for collecting language data from schoolchildren

As described elsewhere in this volume (pp 3, 5-60), a major part of the Languages of London Project has been the interpretation of data provided by London boroughs on languages spoken by their pupils. This in turn has raised issues about the quality of the data obtained. In order to explore ways in which the process of collecting accurate data on pupils' languages could be improved, we collaborated in the drafting of a questionnaire which could be tested on a sample of pupils.

Similar questionnaires, designed to elicit information about languages from pupils, already exist. For example, the University of Reading's Language Information Centre produced a useful one a few years ago, and a questionnaire was trialled in some inner London schools during the eighties. Our questionnaire was specifically designed for use among secondary schoolchildren and to be completed by pupils themselves during a single lesson and with minimal supervision from teachers. However, teachers would need to check the completed questionnaires and, using the checklist (see below), might need to obtain further information from certain pupils.

The most recent version of the questionnaire used comprised Section A, Parts 1 and 2, and Section B, a checklist. Section A, Part 1 is reproduced overleaf. Section A, Part 2 of the questionnaire consisted of two series of questions which may be summarized as follows: (i) *At home, I usually speak to my mother / my father / my guardian / my brother(s) / my sister(s) / my grandparents /my uncles/aunts / my friends / my neighbour in* .... and (ii) *At home, my mother / my father / my guardian / my brother(s) / my sister(s) / my grandparents / my uncles/aunts / my friends / my neighbours usually speak(s) to me in*...
In the period 1995-97, versions of this questionnaire were tested on more than 200 children aged between 11 and 14 attending schools in Westminster . The questionnaire has also been circulated for comment among various people concerned with education in London. Further trialling should include primary schoolchildren, but this would of course require some adaptation of the questionnaire.

The findings

In Questions 3a-3c our purpose was simply to encourage pupils to record that they had some knowledge of other languages rather than to seriously assess their degree of competence in them. The addition of a middle possibility between 'well' and 'a little' could of course have elicited more detailed responses than were actually obtained.

The purpose of Question 5 was to elicit information which might be relevant for the checklist (see below). Questions 6 and 7 were added at the suggestion of teachers taking part in the survey with a view to making completion of the questionnaire more interesting for pupils. They served that purpose well, with most children responding to both these questions, indicating a greater interest in languages they do not currently speak than might have been expected. Unfortunately there is insufficient space to discuss their answers in this article.

For some children, completion of Section A, Part 1 provided all the information that was required. For others, Section A, Part 2 proved invaluable, especially where either (a) two or more languages were mentioned in answer to Question 4 or (b) where the teacher suspected that the pupil had some knowledge of another language not mentioned in the answers in Part 1. Five examples of the usefulness of Part 2 are:

(1) A child from a Welsh-speaking home had been assumed by his teachers to be a monolingual English-speaker but completion of the second part revealed that he also spoke Welsh (Cymraeg). The child had spent more of his life in London than in Wales, his English did not noticeably differ from that of his monolingual English-speaking comrades, and he had a common British surname. Whether the child or his parents had not previously been asked about language use at home – or had been asked but, for whatever reason, had not mentioned Welsh – is not known. What is significant is that the total number of schoolchildren in the whole of London recorded as speaking Welsh at home is a mere 66 whereas a company investigating the viability of making the Welsh-speaking channel S4C available in London on cable television recently estimated the number of Welsh-speakers in the wider London area as about 20,000![1] Even if only half of these lived within the boroughs investigated in this survey, it would seem reasonable to assume that there may be more than 2,000 Welsh-speaking schoolchildren in London (rather than 66). It seems certain that Welsh is seriously under-recorded in our data.

(2) Of several children with one parent whose first language is English and the other with a different first language, there were a few whose ability to speak the latter was unknown to their teachers. The English of these children was not noticeably different from that of their monolingual English-speaking colleagues, but it is not clear whether it is for this reason that teachers had not thought to enquire about language use in their home, or whether they had been asked but had not mentioned the use of any other language.

---

[1]   This figure was provided by members of the Department of Welsh at Cardiff University in 1998.

Experimental questionnaire tested in some Westminster schools in 1995-97

name_____   _____

Section A, Part 1

1a. What languages have you learned at school? ....

....

1b. Do you go to any language classes outside school?   No [__]   Yes   [__]

1c. If you answered Yes, which language(s) are you learning?..

....

2. What other languages do you understand?..

....

3a. Which language(s) can you **speak well**?..

   Which language(s) can you **speak a little**?..

3b. Which language(s) can you **read well**?..

   Which language(s) can you **read a little**?..

3c. Which language(s) can you **write well**?..

   Which language(s) can you **write a little**?..

4. Which languages are spoken in your home?..

....

5. If English is spoken at home, what kind of English is this? (for example, London English, Jamaican English,

Yorkshire English, etc. ....

....

6. What other language(s) would you like to learn?..

....

7. Do you know a few words of any other language spoken by your friends in this class? If so, which

language(s)?..

....

[For Section A, Part 2 of this questionnaire, see p 87.]

(3) In several cases, the use of two languages other than English was reported. Some children of Moroccan parentage said they used Arabic, Berber, and some English at home. Faced with a situation where they felt they were required to name a single home language, such children and/or their parents might reply "Arabic" because they feel this has more status than Berber. This may be partly because "Berber" is considered a somewhat pejorative term but also because a child might know that the names of the actual languages covered by the term "Berber" would be unfamiliar to teachers. (As indicated elsewhere in this volume, the problem might be solved by the introduction of Tamazigh as a more acceptable cover name for this group of languages.)

(4) An unusual case was that of a child who mentioned four languages in answer to Question 3a: Aku, English, Spanish and Wolof. His parents were known to come from the Gambia where both Aku (the Gambian name for Krio) and Wolof are spoken but the mention of Spanish seemed unlikely. However, use of Section A, Part 2 revealed that the child's mother had left the household and his father now lived with a Spanish woman who divided her time between London and Spain where the pupil spent all his school holidays.

(5) A 12-year old girl from Congo (ex-Zaire) initially listed three languages as those spoken in her home: Lingala, French and English. As she sought to complete Part 2 of the questionnaire, it became apparent that she was experiencing some difficulty. In discussion it emerged that one reason for this was that she used all three of these languages, in varying proportions, with her father, brothers and sisters (and both French and Lingala with her mother). In further discussion she revealed, with some reluctance, that she also knew and occasionally spoke two other languages with certain relatives and other people from Congo (ex Zaire): Kiluba and what she called Kimongo. (Subsequent research suggests that Kimongo is probably the Kiluba name for the language normally known by its speakers as Lomongo.) Her reluctance to name the latter pair of languages seemed to indicate that she perceived these as having low status or expected others to do so. This case is important for two reasons. First, as with Berber, it indicates that languages whose speakers consider them to have low status are liable to be seriously under-reported. Secondly, this information could only be elicited from the child by someone familiar with the names of the principal languages of the country concerned. In other words, even though use of a questionnaire such as the one presented here would tend to produce more detailed information than is currently provided by most boroughs, some relevant linguistic information is liable to escape notice.

With the single exception of Westminster,[2] data supplied by LEAs name only one language per child. This reflects an assumption that only one language is spoken in each home. However, as some of the above examples indicate, there are many instances where this is not the case. Use of the questionnaire also showed that, even when just one language other than English was used in the home, there was often some use of English and/or another language as well, especially between siblings.

The checklist which follows (Section B) was intended for use by whoever administered the questionnaire with a view to eliminating any problems which might arise when analysing the data before leaving the class. This proved adequate for all the pupils on whom the questionnaire was tested. However, the alphabetical list of languages (*this volume*, pp 15-58) suggests that, for London as a whole, a number of other responses need to be added. One such is Eritrean which, in most cases, probably refers to Tigrinya but which in some cases may merely indicate the child's country of origin.

Conclusions

The quality of language data collected from schoolchildren could be significantly improved if the process of collecting the data is consistent across LEAs and is based on a positive attitude to multilingualism within schools so that children and their parents are encouraged to respond openly and with confidence. The use by LEAs of a questionnaire such as the one presented here could lead to such an improvement. However, the collection of accurate data also depends on those people collecting the data having some awareness of the responses which they might expect to elicit from children and/or parents from particular ethnolinguistic groups. This awareness should include some familiarity with the identification and correct use of language names and an understanding of how proficiency in a particular language can be overstated or understated depending on the status which that language is perceived to have in the host community.

There is certainly scope for further refinement of the questionnaire. As noted above, there is also a need to adapt it for use with pupils in primary schools. Furthermore, any checklist accompanying the questionnaire would have to be revised periodically to take account of the arrival of previously unrepresented ethnolinguistic groups.

For Baker's biographic details, see p 59 (above).

After working in Westminster for ten years, Antony Sanderson is now responsible for coordinating provision for pupils with English as an additional language in Surrey.

Both authors would welcome comments relating to this article and particularly to the collection of language data in schools and the use of questionnaires. They can be contacted as follows:

Philip Baker   pb@soas.ac.uk (e-mail)

Antony Sanderson   01737 272137   (tel)
                    01737 765437   (fax)

---

[2]   Since 1996, the collection of language data in Westminster allows for two languages used at home to be recorded.

Section B – Checklist

Check that all languages mentioned as being spoken in Section A, Part 1, are also mentioned in Part 2.

If the name of a country is given as the name of a language anywhere in Section A – e.g. "Nigerian language", "Ghana", etc. – ask the child if they can supply the name of the language. If they cannot do this, try to obtain some additional information such as the name of a town or area within the country where the language is spoken.

If, in Section A, the respondent claims to speak any of the languages named below, please use the guidance notes below:

Arabic: Ask respondent to specify which variety of Arabic by country and record as, e.g. Arabic (Egyptian), Arabic (Moroccan) or Maghrebi, etc. If the country mentioned is Morocco or Algeria, also enquire whether the respondent has any knowledge of Berber (and, if so, see Berber below).

Bengali: If Sylheti was not mentioned, ask if respondent also speaks/understands Sylheti. If literacy in either of these languages was indicated, try to establish which is spoken in the home and whether this is the same as the language they write. (It may be that Sylheti is the spoken language and Bengali the written language.)

Berber: Ask respondent to identify which Berber language if possible, e.g. Tamazight, Tamasheq, Tachelhait, ... (there are several others). If unable to do this, ask for the name of a town or area where it is spoken.

Bosnian: Check whether this refers to Croatian (written with the Roman alphabet) or Serbian (written with the Cyrillic (Russian) alphabet).

Chinese: Ask whether the Chinese spoken at home is Cantonese, Hakka, Mandarin, or some other variety and record this as the language spoken and/or understood. If literacy in Chinese is indicated in Section A, do **not** ask which variety is written because all of these share a common written form.

Creole (Patois/Patwa): First, determine if this relates to a language spoken outside the UK and, if so, record this as part of the answer, e.g. Jamaican Patois, Mauritian Creole, etc. (If the territory named is Dominica, Grenada, St Lucia, or Trinidad, ask respondent whether this is an English Creole (Patois) or a French Creole (Patois) and record as, e.g. Dominican English Creole, St Lucian French Creole, etc.) If the pupil is unaware of this being spoken outside the UK, record as "Patwa (London)".

English: If pronunciation is other than London English, supplementary questions may be asked, e.g. does anyone in the household speak a regional (Geordie?) or overseas variety (Jamaican?) of English.

French: If the child or his/her parents are not from French-speaking Europe, enquire about place of origin. If the response is Mauritius or the Seychelles, check whether French or Creole French is the language spoken.

Gaelic: Investigate whether this is Irish or Scottish Gaelic and record as such.

Irish: Enquire whether this means Irish Gaelic or Irish English and record as such.

Kosovan: Check whether the language used is Albanian (Shqipe).

Patwa / Patois - see **Creole** above.

Panjabi: If ability to read or write Panjabi is indicated, enquire which script is used: Arabic (i.e. same as Urdu) or Gurmukhi.

Scottish: Check whether Scottish Gaelic (pronounced Gallic) or Scottish English (Scots) is meant and record as such.

Index

For additional references to countries, see the world map on p 10 and the list of territories/languages on pp 59-60. For the importance of individual languages within each borough, see Table 5 (p 12) and the maps between pages 12 and 58.

91

92